# The Trump Bible

King Donald Version

Copyright © 2018 Peregrin Wood

All rights reserved.

ISBN: 1986592022
ISBN-13: 978-1986592024

# DEDICATION

The creator of the universe was great, really. We're big fans. Never been bigger. Even the universe needed development, though. The creator isn't winning any more. But hey, no one ever got anything done without having a lot of critics standing on the sidelines, explaining why things can't get done. So, we give thanks to Donald Trump for inspiring this new gospel, putting his faith into action.

And more importantly, to the people who are ready to Make America Great Again, we offer our appreciation. They've been a tremendous, very tremendous, source of inspiration. There's no one who has proven to be a greater source of inspiration, as examples of what can be accomplished when we put our critical minds off to the side and just pray on our problems for a spell.

# CONTENTS

|   | About This Book | i |
|---|---|---|
| 1 | Trump Genesis | 1 |
| 2 | Trump Exodus | 5 |
| 3 | Trump Leviticus | 15 |
| 4 | Trump Numbers | 18 |
| 5 | Trump Deuteronomy | 21 |
| 6 | Trump Josh | 25 |
| 7 | Trump Judges | 29 |
| 8 | Trump Lamentations | 32 |
| 9 | Trump Proverbs | 35 |
| 10 | Trump Obadiah | 39 |
| 11 | Trumpzekiel | 41 |
| 12 | Trump Nahum | 43 |
| 13 | Trump Zacharia | 45 |
| 14 | Trump Malachi | 47 |
| 15 | Gospel of Trump | 49 |
| 16 | Trump Romans | 78 |
| 17 | Trump Timothy | 82 |

PEREGRIN WOOD

| 18 | Trump Corinithians | 84 |
| 19 | Trump Colossians | 87 |
| 20 | Trump Titus | 91 |
| 21 | Trump Jude | 93 |
| 22 | Trump Revelations | 95 |

# ABOUT THIS BOOK

Who wrote the Trump Bible?

One might fairly assume that the person who wrote the Trump Bible is Donald Trump himself. Certainly, the aggressively loose, non-linear, style of writing suggests that this is the case. The book appears to follow the example established by Thomas Jefferson, who wrote his own version of the Christian Bible in order to reflect his own beliefs.

Donald Trump has not openly acknowledged writing the Trump Bible. Then again, he is known to have often used pseudonyms in his communications, sometimes even calling up journalists pretending to be his own PR agent.

There is, however, no direct evidence proving that Donald Trump is the author of the Trump Bible. The manuscript was found on the sidewalk outside of Trump Tower in Manhattan, printed on paper, wrapped in brown paper and tied with twine. This plain format does not match Trump's favored style of overwrought luxury.

One possibility is that the text was dictated by Trump, then heavily edited by a ghostwriter, as happened with all of the books that officially carry Donald Trump's name. It is also possible that the book was written by someone entirely unconnected to Trump, seeking to merge his identity with the well-known religious text.

Christian Trump voters may consider another possibility: That the Trump Bible was written by the eternal creator of the universe, come to Earth in order to update its religious teachings for Americans in the wake of the 2016 elections.

Some may wish to dismiss the Trump Bible as "fake", but in these days of fake news reported as fact, who is to judge whether this version of the Bible is genuine? Readers will be capable of judging its truth for themselves.

I didn't write this book. No one named Peregrin Wood

did. I am putting my name on the book, because hey, when else am I going to get to see my name in print? Mainly, though, I want to make the point clear that, although this book is called the Trump Bible, and it often appears to be written using the voice of Donald Trump, and the name Trump has been plastered on every chapter, just as Trump would like to do, it almost certainly was not written by Donald Trump.

When, after all, has Donald Trump ever written a document of this length? It's short by Bible standards, not even bothering to include all 26 books of the traditional Christian Bible. Nonetheless, it's long by Trump standards. Until recently, 144 characters was his limit.

If Donald Trump succeeds in gaining a second term as President of the United States, this book may turn out to be the most theologically important work since Dianetics. With just a little bit more than one year in office, Trump has already changed the American nation in ways that would have been unimaginable two years ago. Why can't he do the same for Christianity, the religion that most of his followers follow?

In 2016, the majority of those Americans who follow Christianity also overwhelmingly voted for Donald Trump. So, is there a separation between Christianity and Trumpism any more?

Read on. Perhaps the Trump Bible can help us gain a clear vision of the new Trumptianity.

# 1 TRUMP GENESIS

So, as you all know, God created heaven and earth first thing. Bold move.

Problem was, God didn't give the earth any form. It was void, all void. Sad.

There was darkness everywhere, too. You couldn't see a thing. If you wanted a lightbulb, well, you couldn't get one anywhere. The business environment was terrible. There was no innovation anywhere. You literally could not create any jobs. Too much regulation.

God was low energy. Sleepy. He just moved around on the surface, on top of the water. It was a holiday at a water park, folks. A very dark water park.

After a long time, nobody knows how long it was, but it was very very long, believe me, God got bored. So, God said, "Hey, could somebody give me a light here?"

Wouldn't you know it? Someone brought God a light. True story.

God saw the light, and thought it was good, because he was into centralized planning. A cosmic socialist, am I right?

Then, God divided the light from the darkness. He was picking winners and losers, stifling free the market.

Then, God started exceeding his executive authority, saying he wanted some land. That first land was America, which is why we say America First.

But then, God choked, and he left the Earth with three quarters water. 75% wet! I can tell you that if I created the universe, I would have made it 110% earth.

So, next, God set up the Environmental Protection Agency, with a whole bunch of species nobody ever heard of. Each one of them had their own territory, where no one would be allowed to build hotels.

Consider the Southern New Jersey lesser beach grass. You ever heard of it? Me neither. But would they let me move it to the side a little to build my Trump Casino at Stone Harbor? No. The beach grass huggers rigged it against me.

After that, the evening and the morning were the third day. The second day was for playing golf.

God had this very nice garden made, which was next to a luxury hotel. It had these great lights in the firmament, all gilded with extra crystals. You have to create the best.

Trouble was that God didn't have any customers. Very bad. Not his fault, but I would have done it differently.

So, God made a man and a woman, so that he could have a real estate market. That was pretty good. Not great. So-so. I would created millions of people to come to my hotel openings. Unprecedented. No one has done so much. I have the photographs to prove it.

In order to expand the real estate market, God told the man and the woman to have lots of children. He told them, "Look! I've given you every herb bearing seed, and every tree, and every bit of meat. Have at it! The food's on me. The rooms are going to cost you, though."

God had just one other rule: If the man and the woman wanted to enjoy the nice fruit as part of their complementary breakfasts, that's great. Just don't take the fruit up to your room, because if you do, it will encourage

# THE TRUMP BIBLE

ants and other vermin to spread.

Did they listen? Of course not. The woman wanted to sleep in. The man thought that he could make her happy by bringing her a piece of fruit for a late morning snack.

Like Ronald Reagan said, "Trust but verify." God had a surveillance camera installed in their hotel suite, and saw the woman eating a banana, and leaving the peel out on the bathroom counter.

So, God went up to their room and confronted them about it. The guy was like, "Please, don't hurt me! She ate the fruit!" You should have seen him whining. It was funny.

God is a nice guy, but he's a realist. He made a deal, and they both broke it. He kicked them out of the Garden Hotel, and told them to never come back.

That was strong. We need more leadership like that. We have to secure our borders, God said, and if people can't come here legally, and respect our laws, then they ought to just leave, and stay out. That's why God put a great big wall all around America. I'm talking big like you've never seen. Believe me.

God wasn't going to just build them another luxury hotel to stay in, either. No. But he's a nice guy. He told them that they would have to work for a living. No more loafing around. He made the man and the woman build the wall for him.

All that work was good for their character, too, except if you count this guy named Abel. He died. That much is true, but his supporters accused his brother Cain of killing him. It was fake news. Cain had the worst media ever. He was punished, and his descendants, too, with things like bad childbirth, which makes a whole lot of sense, if you think about it. Cain didn't have good DNA.

Anyway, Cain's kids started spreading all over the place, making lots of babies. Of course, you know what's going to happen when there's inbreeding like that. Let me tell you, those people were some bad hombres.

Don't get me wrong, I'm sure some of them were nice, but most of them were climbing over the wall, sneaking back into America. They were violating our laws, raping, murdering, taking people's jobs.

So, God said, "You know what I'm gonna do? I'm gonna flood the shit out of them." They didn't know what hit them. The lying media complained. "Oh, what about the babies?" God said, "Sometimes you gotta be tough, you know? It'll teach them a lesson."

There was this one guy, though, who was smart enough to hire a good lobbyist ahead of time. Good businessman. So, he arranged for his family to be put on a private yacht to ride out the floods in comfort.

You should have seen this place. It was great. Amazing. Velvet upholstery. Private movie theater. It was the best yacht ever. All the amenities. Golf on the upper deck. At the end of the ride, it came with its own private rainbow. Members only.

Wouldn't you know it, an inspector from the Environmental Protection Agency came along and declared the yacht to be a vital habitat, and made the guy keep a bunch of mating pairs of animals in stowage so they wouldn't go extinct. God said, "If the animals couldn't survive a global catastrophic flood, they're weak! What do you want to do, encourage them?"

The EPA inspector threatened to file a lawsuit, though. So, what could God do? You can't run world-flooding business like that, with people nitpicking all the time. It was harder than God thought it would be.

So, God told this guy and his family, "You're a great guy. Seriously. Good genetics. Go on and make lots of babies, and make sure to live the right away, according to traditional American values. No more floods. Promise."

That's just what happened, too, until God decided that this guy's family was rotten after all. They really needed to learn a lesson. Nasty people. Real sinners. We'll get to that later, though.

THE TRUMP BIBLE

For now, rainbows.

# 2 TRUMP EXODUS

After things dried out, people made babies again, and they spread out. Some were in a place called Israel. Beautiful place. I have a golf course there.

Ruben, Simeon, Levi, Judah, Issachar, Zebulon, Benjamin, Daniel, Naphtali, Gad, and Asher were all club members. They had a lot of children. One guy named Jacob had 70 kids.

Problem was, these Israelis left their own club. They went over into Egypt, which as a different country, with its own borders. There was no wall on the border between Israel and Egypt, though. There was no security. Sad!

The pharaohs of Egypt were job producers. They gave the people of Israel many jobs. Unemployment was low. They were making bricks, farming, building treasure city. Egypt was great.

I love Egypt. I hug Egyptians all the time. But Egypt made a big mistake. Big. They tried to force Hebrew women to perform abortions, and kill babies. That was bad. Very bad.

So, the Jews living in Egypt decided they needed to

reassert their Judeo-Christian values, and get back to their Homeland, where there would be effective screening at the airports.

God had made this campaign promise, you see. Said he was going to protect the children of Israel and make them prosper. Being God is hard, though. It's harder than he thought it would be. Not easy.

God's advisors looked at the Google analytics. He did some A/B tests. He had the best data, and decided that he could improve his support in the right demographics if he brought back the promise. It was time to make Israel great again.

So, God lit himself on fire. It was a big fire. You never saw a bigger one. Huge.

God yelled at this guy named Mo. "Hey, look at me! I'm a burning bush, right? Go and get your people. We're going on a trip back to Israel."

Mo shouted back, "Hey, I saw how bad things are in Egypt. People there are crying. Their leaders are terrible. Sorrows, big league. But you know, I think the Jews are just upset about last year's election. Trying to delegitimize it. Who am I to tell the pharaoh his business? He's a very successful man, a job creator."

Then God said, "Look, and I often say this, I am what I am, you know what I mean? So just tell people I said that there's this place with a whole lot of milk. It's unprecedented in all of the history of Israel how much milk there is there. Honey too. You never saw so many beehives. Big. That's where we're going, okay?"

God continued, "So, when you talk to the pharaoh, I'm going to make sure he doesn't listen to you, and won't let you leave Egypt, because I want you to get a bunch of people to leave Egypt."

Mo was like, "What? That doesn't make any sense. Why not just be nice and convince the pharaoh to let us leave?"

God said, "Believe me. I know The Art of the Deal. I

am the best negotiator. I get all the best deals. I'm going to make up a nickname for the pharaoh. Call him Little Ramses. Call him Pyramid Man. Make him refuse to give you what you want. Make him dangerous. Best way to get a good deal on leaving Egypt. Also, here's a stick that becomes a snake. Cool, huh?"

Mo had to be alone for a while after that. Collect his thoughts. Went out to the desert to kiss a guy named Aaron. It's okay. The GLBLTQ people love me. Biggest fans.

Pharaoh had very bad security, so Aaron and Mo walked right up to him, and said, "Let my people go!"

Pharaoh said, "No," because God had hardened his heart.

So Mo and Aaron stood there for a second. Looked at each other. They walked back to the place where the bush had caught fire. They thought, "This is a plan?"

"You should have thrown that stick at him," Aaron said. Did you remember to bring it?

Mo slapped his forehead — a terrible leader.

"Don't worry," Aaron said. I've got a big rod. A great rod. It swallows up all the other rods. A great snake.

Aaron and Mo went back to the pharaoh, and this time had a rod, and they filled up pools of water with blood, and there were also a lot of frogs, and lice, and other vermin.

Eventually, Egypt got tired of all this rod nonsense, and let the Jews go up to the land of Canaan, because the land of Canaan did not have a secure border, and the Jews took all the jobs from the Canaanites, and were rapists and criminals, which just goes to show you.

When pharaoh heard how good Mo and Aaron had it in the land of Canaan, however, he decided to follow and get what he could for himself. The waters of the Red Sea rose up and swallowed him and his armies, though, which just goes to show you that climate change is nothing new, so we should burn a lot of coal.

THE TRUMP BIBLE

Now, on the way to the land of Canaan, Mo and Aaron and their followers decided to camp at the base of a mountain. Mo wanted to go up the mountain, however, because he had heard that there was a really classy resort up there, with a five star golf course, and some opportunities for a little money laundering on the side.

It was a scam. There was just a big pile of tablets up there, with a bunch of rules.

Mo was an enterprising guy, though, so he brought down the tablets, and he stood up in front of everybody, and he shouted, "Listen up! Things are going to be different around here from not on! I got some things to say."

Command Number 1: No graffiti!

Command Number 2: The media hates me. If you hear them spreading rumors about me, it's fake news!

Command Number 3: Everyone here needs to be working six days a week, but you're going to get paid for just five days. You should be grateful that you have a job!

Command Number 4: From now on, we're all saying Merry Christmas! None of this Communist "Happy Holidays" nonsense!

Command Number 5: In America, we worship God, not government, so you've got to be Christian, okay?

Command Number 6: You cannot have any Republican Party leader before me.

Command Number 7: Don't take the name of Trump in vain, right? It's trademarked.

Command Number 8: I can shoot someone in the middle of 5th Avenue, and my supporters will not abandon me.

Command Number 9: If I hire someone to do a big project for me, but I decide I don't like the way they did the work, I don't have to pay them. Bye bye!

Command Number 10: If there is another man's wife, I can just go up and kiss her and grab her by the pussy, because I'm a celebrity, and people will let you do anything.

"One more thing," said Mo, "Though this isn't a command, it's just the truth. I'm on my third wife now, but a man like me isn't so good at the marriage thing. There are all these beautiful girls I just walk into at the Miss Universe pageant, and any one of them is mine if I covet them. Believe me."

And the people stood far off, and didn't quite know what to think.

"It's family values," said Mo. "Also, God made another command. He said that if you make a church, you shouldn't cut the stones you use to make it. Why? I don't know. It's a command. Isn't that good enough for you?"

One final thing: You all can buy slaves. Who wouldn't. I love slaves. Slaves are good business.

If you buy a slave, and give that slave a wife, that wife really belongs to you, and even if you set your slave free, the slave's wife and her children are your property. If the slave doesn't want to lose his wife, then you can just smash a hole through the slave's ear, and then the slave will belong to you forever.

What are you going to do? It's traditional morality. You're not against traditional morality, are you?

Look, if you're going to be respected, sometimes you've got to be tough. So, if you've got a son who says something nasty about you, you just have to take him out into a public plaza, maybe Central Park, and smash his body with stones until he's dead. It's not a crime. It's just the law of God, am I right? Who are we to question the Bible?

Also, if you have an ox, and that ox gets hurt, call a good lawyer.

Kill all the witches! I hate witches. Never met an honest witch.

Don't get me angry, because when my wax gets hot, I will go around killing people I'm angry with. I'll cut you up with a sword. What are you going to do about it? I've got

# THE TRUMP BIBLE

the word of God on my side!

You aren't allowed to say anything bad about any gods, or about the President of the United States, which is pretty much the same thing, if you ask me. But hey, the Bible says so, so you have to do it, right?

There's a problem, though. Big problem. Right here in this book of Exodus, in the Bible itself, and therefore not open to questioning, it says that people aren't supposed to accept gifts. "Take no gift," it says, "for the gift blinds the wise and perverts the words of the righteous".

That's Fake Scripture, though. So, I'll keep on taking my emoluments, which are directed to my business which is run my wonderful sons, Eric and Donald Jr., who I promise never to talk to about business when we meet behind closed doors, and my word is my bond, honest, I won't do it, and if I do go to visit my business holdings and powerful politicians and foreign dignitaries and executives who are making big payments just so happen to be there, and we just accidentally start to talk about business dealings, and I happen to say something like "Hey, I just made you guys all a lot richer," after getting a big tax loophole for rich guys passed through Congress, well, who is to say that's unethical?

Look, I just wrote a new part of the scripture that says, "It's totally okay for President Donald Trump to accept gifts, because the President cannot obstruct justice or break the law." There you go. Now it's in the Bible, and you can't question it. See? I'm a very holy person, and I take the Bible very seriously. So, where's the gifts, friends?

Okay, here's another problem. Some people, want to cause trouble, they look at the book of Exodus, and say, hey, there are three holidays that are allowed by this part of the Bible:

There's a feast of flatbread. So, we can have quesadillas or something. As I already said last year, the Hispanics love me, so that's good.

There's a feast of harvest, and I pardoned the turkey.

So far, so good.

Then there's a feast of ingathering, which is when you gather stuff out of the fields. So, look, I was raised in real estate, not in farm labor, which, let me point out, has a lot of nasty immigrants, very dangerous people who are raping and murdering a lot of people, like did I mention that scary gang in Long Island? I'm sure that has something to do with this, so we need a wall! A big wall to keep the Mexicans out! You have never seen anything like this wall before. Going to be great, and make America great again. So big!

Where was I? Right. Ingathering. What is that? I mean, okay, you have a harvest festival, and then another festival when you get all the "labors out of the field". Isn't that the same thing as harvest? I don't get it. Doesn't make sense.

So, the thing is, I noticed that the Bible is afraid to say "Christmas". Not once! The Bible writers, they keep on talking about "ingathering" and feasts, but they don't every say "Christmas". Sad.

It's because of liberal college professors, who have banned Christmas. It's true! I saw them in New Jersey, on September 11, 2001, banning Christmas. They were celebrating in the streets, and smashing the baby Jesus.

Well, now that I'm President, we are all going to say "Merry Christmas!" Or else! No "happy three festivals" any more, get it?

It's disgusting, how people like Rosie O'Donnell are part of the Bible's War On Christmas, defending this "holy book" that doesn't mention "Christmas" even once. Worse than Starbucks!

But now that I am the winner of the 2016 election, and did I mention that I won that election with an overwhelming majority of the popular vote? Oh yes! There were 20 million Mexicans who voted illegally, and that's been proven, but I won the election by 400 million popular votes. True!

Anyway, I was saying, doesn't Melania look great? So,

now that I'm President, I'm renegotiating the Bible. Getting a better deal. Got a filibuster-proof majority. So now, as you can see, "Christmas" is finally in the Bible!

See, I just said it again. Christmas, Christmas, Christmas! I make America great every time I say it, and no welfare queen taking money from the National Endowment for the Arts on public lands can do anything about it, can she? Out you go Omarosa! You're fired!

Look, I told you, and CNN won't report this, but I'm going to say it again: The Bible says "You will not bow down to their gods, nor serve them, nor do after their works, but shall utterly overthrow them, and destroy their images." You see? It's right there. That's why I say that radical Islamic terrorists are out to destroy America and our way of life, and the Boy Scouts, and the Happy Meal. They hate the Happy Meal.

So, I will stand in front of this Christmas tree in front of the White House, and talk about how Jesus is the Lord and Saviour of the the federal government (Steve Bannon said to put in that extra U in Savior, because it gives it that Jurrasic Park panache) and there isn't anything anyone is going to do about it.

They keep on complaining about "separation of church and state". Keep it separate, they say! I say to them, separate yourself!

Another thing. People keep on saying, "We need healthcare! We're entitled! Medicare for all!" Have you read your Bible? Really? It says right here in the Bible that God is going to take away sickness from everybody who follows him, right?

So, I'm just saying, the sick must be some kind of godless liberals if they're sick! I'm bringing you super-low health care costs: Just pray to Jesus and be healed. Is that not good enough for you? What, you think you deserve some platinum plan when you're not even taking the free prayer option I've offered you? I don't think so.

Immigrants. That's the other thing. I have a mandate

from God, who delivered me a 400 million popular vote victory, to get rid of the immigrants. The ones from Haiti, they've all got AIDS anyway, right? So look, in the Bible, God cleaned the land of Hivites and Canaanites, add Hittites. No foreigners! This is our Homeland!

Okay. Enough commandments. I lost my place. Where did the story go next?

Right. There was a mountain. Big mountain. Mo wet there for 40 days days and 40 nights. He was playing golf.

Now, the lying press, they're going to tell you that's playing too much golf. It's true, when Barack Obama was President, he spent way too much time playing golf. But Mo, a 40-day golf vacation while his followers were wandering around in the desert, that was a sign of executive clarity. Real leadership.

Besides, God was like a devouring fire up there. Like in California, you know, but totally natural. Not due to climate change, which was a thing they made up in China, a hoax to make us stop making muscle cars in Detroit.

And God said to Mo, get yourself a really fine penthouse apartment in Manhattan, and get some oil for the light, and spices for anointing oil, and some really nice cranberry-scented candles, and onyx stones, and stones to be set in the ephod, and gold leaf to cover every square inch of the rest of the place, and make it a sanctuary, and I will come and visit you there, that I may dwell among you when I am in town.

And God said, I know I told you before to make a bunch of stuff out of shittim wood, like an ark, and staves, and things like that, but on second thought, use something else besides shittim wood, because every time the middle school children among you are told about the shittim wood, they will giggle, and I am not going to have that.

You have to make curtains to go with it all, to match the décor. Why are we talking about curtains when we're out in the middle of the desert up on the mountain playing golf for 40 days? I have no idea. Just go with it, okay? But if you want to have nice curtains, just check with Melania, because she is really eager to have something to do, like redecorate the White House for Christmas with a hall of white-spray-painted twigs with lighting coming up from the floor like a scene from The Shining or something. I totally think that counts as fifty taches of gold. 49 at a minimum.

Then, I want some extra light virgin olive oil – not that organic stuff they sell at Whole Foods, which is owned by the Washington Post now – fake news!

So, okay, you know, a lot of people say I do not like the GLGBTQ people. Wrong! We had a party with these new decorations, and there was this friend of mine Aaron – a great guy. Really great. He brought his friends, and they were wearing lots of rings and breastplates and girdles, and they ministered to me in the office, and I was totally comfortable with it. Everyone noticed how much I was loving the rainbow then. The curious girdle of the ephod, I'm just saying, it was huge! The gays love me.

And then God said to Mo, gather all your followers, and have them go out and take a sword and cut up all of their brothers and companions and neighbors. Don't worry. It's okay to go off killing people. They weren't staying with the true religion. That's what the Constitution says. Freedom means kill people when they aren't in the right religion. There's a clause in there somewhere about that.

Look, God is jealous. Jealousy is good. It's like greed, in that movie with that guy Gordon Gecko. Don't worry about the details. Just go with it.

Also, don't heat your homes on Sundays. If you do, that's a big sin.

Okay, Exodus! I think we're done here. Moving on. Next item on the agenda!

# 3 TRUMP LEVITICUS

Look, if we need to talk about it, there's this thing you've got to do, which, I don't like to talk about, but you need to burn a lot of bulls and sprinkle their blood everywhere. Doesn't smell good, to be honest.

So, when you do this, you'd better just do it on the White House lawn somewhere, maybe next to that old magnolia tree that Melania ordered to be cut down because it was blocking her view. Yeah, that's a good spot.

But if you want to barbecue some of the pigeons we have in DC, a whole lot of them in Lafayette Park, you have to just take them and wring their necks, and cut their wings off, but don't cut the body. Here's the secret: You want to brine the pigeons, so that they get really moist and tender before you grill them. Trust me, use more salt than you think you need, and add some black pepper, with some really fine flour and some more olive oil, so the skin is nice and crispy.

Or, you could have a White House staffer bring in some Happy Meals, if it's been a really long day, and John Kelly is trying to tell everybody how everything is going to be. Just sneak out and have a little meeting on the side, and get some chicken McNuggets and dip your finger in the barbecue sauce seven times, and sprinkle it on the McNuggets just so. The sanctuary in the hallway next to the Oval Office is a good place for this. John Kelly never thinks to look there.

So, here's the thing. People like to talk a lot about the mistakes you make. They call you unclean. They say you don't talk right, or you do outrageous things. Is it true? They say that you're dirty just because someone next to you swears about something, and are you guilty about these things? No.

Here's what it's really all about: Hillary Clinton is just upset about losing the election by 400 million votes. Unprecedented victory! Crooked Hillary is just looking for an excuse for being a big loser. So, all you need to do is go and get a lamb, and kill it and burn it, and it's all good. No harm, no foul!

There are a whole lot of recipes out there, about what you should kill and cook and eat if you've done something wrong. I'm not saying I've done something wrong, but hey, what if I did, in theory, do something wrong?

I could take a censer, and put fire therein, and wring the necks of lambs, and all that, but I've talked to my lawyers, and they tell me that I can just pardon myself, even before I've been convicted of doing anything.

So, the important thing is not to eat any rabbits, because they don't have cloven hooves. Actually, they don't have hooves at all, except for the jackelopes, but you get my point.

Another thing is that, if you get a funny looking rash, don't worry about whether you have health care coverage. Just go show it to a priest. They are going to give you the best health care, under my plan. The best. Period. You've never seen health care like this before. Unprecedented.

No lobster in the White House. That's my rule. The problem with lobster? When you eat them, and you crack open their shells, the butter splatters everywhere, and you have to hire people to clean the house. Very hard to get out of the carpet.

As long as we're talking about lobsters and carpets, it's a good time to bring up naked people. So, you should not walk in on the nakedness of your mother, or your mother's sister, or your brother's wife, or your daughter in law, or the nakedness of a woman and her daughter, or of a young girl who you run into in a courtroom while she is waiting for her parents' custody hearing, or of any girls that you should run into while trolling in the local shopping mall, unless you are in Alabama. If you are in Alabama, and you uncover the nakedness of little girls, you should run for the United States Senate.

If you are in Russia, and you uncover the nakedness of young girls who are not your wife, you can get away with it, and should then solicit the services of Russian prostitutes, who will urinate on the bed at your request, if you're into that kind of thing.

You must not eat the flesh of a camel, however, because it doesn't chew cud. After all, we have to set moral limits somewhere.

To eat a pig, however, which has cloven hooves but does not chew its cud, is theoretically forbidden, but, because it's something that we all do anyway, is really okay. Lots of Christian preachers have Sunday barbecues, after all, and we can't go criticizing them. It would impolitic.

About that man lying with man thing, though, because that's written in the Bible, it must be absolutely taken literally. You must persecute gays and lesbians, because you love the Bible a lot, and have no choice but to obey it.

Except for the pork thing. I mean, do you really love the Bible enough to give up hot dogs? Of course not.

# 4 TRUMP NUMBERS

God had a chat with Mo in the wilderness of Sinai, on a cold day in January, saying, "Look at the size of that crowd there! I have never seen a crowd this big, before. It is totally record-breaking, the biggest Sinai crowd that has ever existed, much bigger than the crowd that came when Barack Obama was in the wilderness of Sinai, that's for sure!"

But Satan was among them, in secret, with a camera that appeared to show, through evil witchcraft, that the crowd in the wilderness with God and Mo was rather thin that year, much smaller than had appeared in previous years.

It was a wicked deception of the same kind that Satan had used on September 11, 2001, when I was in New Jersey and saw huge crowds of cheering Muslims celebrating that day's terrorism, although all the news cameras that had been out that day appeared to show that no such crowds had existed.

This same evil once again was visited upon the house of Trump, but in audio form, when a microphone appeared to record me saying that I supported the invasion of Iraq. That interview didn't count! It was Satan, creating a fake audio recording of my voice.

Once again, the Access Hollywood camera that recorded me saying that I like to go up to married women, and grab them by the pussy, and I can get away with doing anything because I'm a celebrity, that was completely fake news, even though I admitted it was real last year. It's all fake, now. It was manufactured by Satan and his camera of lies. How could anyone believe otherwise?

You want to talk about numbers? Okay. Let's talk about numbers. My tax plan, which was passed into law at the end of December 2017, is going to make everyone in the middle class into millionaires. Really!

Under my plan, a family with an annual income of $56,000 will be able to deduct $975,000 from their taxes, and claim a Beemer tax credit of $20,000 for every BMW in their garages. My aides tell me that the average American family owns five BMWs, so right there you get a tax deduction of over one million dollars. Instant millionaire!

Can you believe the Democrats voted against this plan?

The Congressional Budget Office has said that my tax plan will eventually increase the taxes paid by middle class families, while creating big, permanent savings for economic elites and powerful corporations. That's just Satan again, though. You can't believe the nonpartisan CBO, because they are infested with Satan's deceptions.

Believe me.

God said, take the sum of African-American citizens in a state, and when that sum equals or exceeds twenty percent, you shall institute voter ID laws to be enforced in disproportionately African-American districts. And this is the name of this policy that you shall provide: Protection against voter fraud. For Satan created millions of illegal ballots that make it appear that I have not won a victory of 400 million ballots in the popular vote, in order to support his infernal candidate, Crooked Hillary, who if you have been around her, you know smells suspiciously like sulphur.

Such is the word of Alex Jones, of InfoWars, who also declared that the federal government was going to take away everyone's guns two years ago, and informed us all about the secret sex ring operated by Crooked Hillary in the basement of a pizza parlour. By their pepperoni you shall know them.

And the lobbyists of my corporate sponsors shall pitch their projects in the Oval Office, every man with his own big spending project or subsidy. But those lobbyists that did not support my candidacy shall pitch their projects to an intern assisting a deputy assistant secretary of Housing and Urban Development, where their pleas shall receive a fair hearing.

Such is the enumeration of the inhabitants of the swamp. Their corruption is one of the few things we can count on.

# 5 TRUMP DEUTERONOMY

These are the words that Mo said while he was playing golf at this beautiful five-star world class course on this side of the river Jordan in the wilderness, with a restaurant overlooking the plains above the Red Sea. You would not believe how great it is there.

It came to pass that in his 70<sup>th</sup> year of that Mo spoke to all the children of his people, after he had killed a whole bunch of people in a number of cities.

Mo said, You all have lived here long enough. This is a rat trap. I'm working on a deal for some luxury apartments a little distance from here, in the valley where the Canaanites live. It's going to be great.

I know that there are some people who are complaining, and they think that we're going straight into the hands of the Amorites, to be destroyed. These people are just upset that they aren't the leader. I am the leader. Everything they say is bogus. It's a pile of garbage, and it's very unfair.

Believe me. Believe me, it's going to be great, but thanks to the Democrats, you're not going to see the benefits of all our work for another generation. Your kids are going to love it, though. I told you, Barack Obama, was he even born here?

It's like I said: Israel first! We are going to make Israel great again! You can't even imagine how good it's going to be.

There are those among you who said this wouldn't work. Little men. Little men who didn't understand. Believe me, they're not going to make it there with us.

But look, there are all these people just streaming across the borders of Israel. It's a flood! There's chaos, and it's because no one is securing the border. You can't have a country if you don't have borders!

Well, we are coming across the borders too, but the point is, our people were here first. The Zamzummim giants are all gone. Over! Nobody sees them any more.

Now King Sihon of Heshbon, he understands the importance of borders, and won't let us through. The Lord has hardened his heart, and rightly so. I love an obstinate heart. Beautiful!

We attacked him with the mother of all bombs, though. Bye bye, Little Sihon! And we utterly killed all his people, including all their children. Not one was left!

That's how you show strength. People don't understand that these days. You have to be strong! Israel first.

We destroyed a whole lot of people in other cities too. Killing children is righteous. Serves them right for not getting out of our way.

So, God was angry with us before, under the Democrats, and we didn't win anything. Israel just didn't win anymore!

But then, somehow, God wasn't angry with us, and we started winning again. Why did that happen? It's not clear. I think it's because we started establishing some borders.

These cities, many score of them, the people there had high walls. Beautiful walls. You have not seen walls like these walls.

The walls didn't work, and we took the cities anyway.

That's because when you build a wall, you need to not just build high walls, but very very high walls, and that's what I'm going to build now. Unprecedented very high! They're going to be big. So big.

Our nation is great! What nation is there so great as what we have? Not one. We are making Israel great, and we have the best god too. No one has a god like ours.

Are you afraid of God? You should be. That's why I called you all here today, to make them hear my words, and be afraid, and teach your children that fear.

Why fear? It's because you need to perform! I want productivity. That's why we have the strongest economy of all time. You've never seen one stronger.

I brought you out of a hell hole. It was chaos. It was like you were in furnace, it was so bad, but did I bring you here? Yes I did. I won. All the people in Bethpeor, and at the top of Pisgah, and King Og of Bashan, they were low energy.

Then Mo stood and gave a great speech again. You should have seen the audience that was there. It was huge, not that CNN would show it. No, they never showed how big the crowds at Mo's rallies were.

Mo said, In Israel, we don't worship government. We worship God! So, do what I tell you, because these words are from God, not me. Believe me.

Then Mo had another rally, and he said pretty much the same thing. He had a great stump speech.

You have to take what you want, all the good stuff, Mo said to them, and cast out those who had it before. You deserve it, because you are a winner. That's why I'm going to lower your taxes. Don't worry about the losers. We are totally righteous.

The Hittites, and the Girgashites, and the Amorites, and the Canaanites, and the Perizzites, go kill them all, and show no mercy. Don't even rape their women and children. Just kill them all!

We need to show strength, because God will be angry

with you if you show any mercy to any of them. Burn it all down! Fire and fury like you have never seen before!

They're all a bunch of liberals who hate God. They don't understand how great God is, but we're going to show them. Kill them all. We will repay their hatred of god to their faces, and destroy them all, because we remember the commandment: Thou shall not kill… except for all the people I tell you to kill.

Do this, and there's going to be a great health care plan. We're going to come up with health care so good, there won't be any sickness among you. All the evil diseases of the nanny state, they will be gone. Poof! Just like that.

Consume these people! Destroy them! No pity! Your god, after all, is mighty and terrible!

These are wonderful family values. What did I tell you? The Democrats don't get it. They blame you for it. They say you're all a bunch of deplorables, for going out and killing a bunch of cities full of children. They don't understand your righteousness. They think they know better than you.

These elites, they have to go, too. Take what you want. It belongs to you because you're strong and they're weak. Though you may say that it's the power of and might of your hand, remember, it was God who really gave you the power to slaughter all those kids, so don't forget the power of God. Be obedient to God, who destroys nations, and you'll be all set up, though.

Obedience to destruction will bring you the good life. Such is my promise to you. Good times.

Then, after having a lot of other big rallies, Mo died, and you've never seen another guy like that, who had such a mighty hand, in all the great terrorism which Mo showed in the sight of all Israel.

# 6 TRUMP JOSH

With Mo gone, Josh took power. Every place he set foot, that place was given to him by God. Power rules.

So, you know what happened, right? Yes, lots more righteous killing.

God said to Josh the son of Nun, "All the land from the Sinai to the river Euphrates, and all of Asia Minor, that belongs to you and your people. That's Israel! Think big!"

"Josh, as I was with Mo, I will be with you too. Never mind the part where I made Mo die without seeing Israel, which I promised he would see. Forget that part. Never happened. The other stuff, I mean. I swore to give this land unto the fathers of all the people of Israel, but this time, I really mean what I say. Honest."

So Josh had a big rally, and spoke to the Reubenites, and to the Gadites, and to half the tribe of Manasseh, because the other half was a bunch of liberals. Anyway, it was a big rally. It was literally unprecedented. You have never seen so many people, not that the king of Jericho would mention it to his people, because the king of Jericho was fake news.

Josh said to them all, "God tells me that all of this land that other people are living on actually belongs to us. So, we need to be strong! It's time to Make Israel Great Again!"

"By the way, and this is important, I speak for God, and God says that whatever I tell you is goes. It's a command, okay? That means, whoever doesn't follow my commands, and won't listen to me, we're going to kill those people. This is about Judeo-Christian values, after all."

So Josh then sent a couple of spies into Jericho to figure out how the city could be destroyed. A woman there hid them from the king, saying, "We're all totally afraid of you, that your army going to kill us all and destroy the city. We don't win anything in Jericho any more. So, look, just don't kill my family, and then I'll let you go, and you can betray everyone else here, okay."

The spies of Israel thought that was a pretty good deal, so they spun her a yarn about how she could wrap a red cord around her window dressings, and so long as everybody hid in the house during the genocide, they would be okay. Who could blame anybody for killing them if they had the chutzpah to go walking in the streets, though? Everybody gets that killing in the streets is what you have to do to show that you're tough, right?

So, the two men came back to Josh, and told him everything that they knew. Then, Josh sent out a quick little message by a messenger bird. "Just got word back from Little Jericho. Thanks to the lady with the red cord!"

Men from that other half of the tribe of Mannaseh rose up, saying, "Josh, you just compromised the national security of our people with the tweeting of that little bird! You revealed our sources and methods! Now, no one else will ever help us."

Josh spake unto them, saying, "Didn't I tell you that you would be killed if you didn't listen to me?" Then he summoned the Levites, and had them open up the ark of the covenant upon the second half of the tribe of Mannaseh, and the men of Mannaseh in their liberal pride did not close their eyes, and so their faces melted away as the spirits of the ark swirled around them, even as Indiana Jones had foreseen.

Then, all of the people feared Josh, the same way they were afraid of Mo, and they didn't get uppity any longer. They had learned to fear the lord their God forever.

And the next day, Josh got up early in the morning, and cut pieces of skin off all the penises of the men and boys of all the tribes of Israel in a place that forever after was called "The Hill of the Foreskins". Nobody ever went there in pilgrimage after that, though.

"You want milk? You want honey?" Josh said unto the men and boys. "First, you gotta get cut. Hey, I don't make the rules. God said to do it. This is totally healthy, and not at all a sadistic abuse of power. Just remember, if you don't do what I say, I'll have to kill you."

Then, people sat around eating manna, looking at their feet nervously, and trying to pretend that it all never happened.

Josh wasn't done, though. He marched right up to Jericho, and met Speaker Ryan there, and said to him, "Hey, are you with me or against me?"

Then Speaker Ryan thought for a minute, and looked in his pockets for the scruples he was sure he had brought with him, but finding none, replied, "I guess I'm with you, but hey, you've got to take off your shoes so that I look like a principled leader, okay?"

So, Josh took off his shoes, and he led his army marching around the city of Jericho seven times, making a lot of noise until the walls all fell down, and then Josh and his army went into the city and killed everything that they saw. They killed every man, woman and child, and all the farm animals, even the donkeys.

Why did they kill the donkeys? You figure that out.

Anyway, then Josh said, "Take all of the gold and silver out of the accursed place of Jericho, and bring it to my treasury. Oops, I mean to the treasury of God. Yeah, that's it."

But Achan the son of Zerah had taken a nice Babylonian bathrobe and two hundred shekels, and kept it himself. So, Josh said to him, "Confess! You have taken of the accursed Jericho, and failed to give these little treasures to me, I mean, to God!"

So, Achan the son of Zerah confessed, and then Josh took Achan and all of his sons, and his daughters, and his farm animals, even the donkeys, and Josh's soldiers threw stones at them, and then burned them alive.

Why did they kill the donkeys? You figure that out.

So, Josh was finally appeased, and turned from the fierceness of his anger. I mean, God was finally appeased, and turned from the fierceness of his anger.

The next day, Josh went up to the city of Ai, and killed everyone there, all twelve thousand inhabitants, and hung the corpse of the king up in the tree. This was done because of Judeo-Christian values.

There was no word, however, whether they killed the donkeys of Ai.

You get the picture. Lots of cities, lots of killing. Josh and his armies kept on killing entire cities of people until he was an old man, very old. He Made Israel Great Again, and made everyone afraid of him. That's what it takes to be a success. Am I right?

# 7 TRUMP JUDGES

Now after the death of Josh, it came to pass that the children of Israel asked, "Now that we don't have Josh to be afraid of, who is going to judge us, and smite us with stones, and burn us alive?"

Someone asked, "What about Kenaz, Caleb's younger brother? Wasn't he the choice of Josh?"

But then, Judah stood forward and said, "No, that doesn't count. We have to let the people decide."

Then, Judah decided. I decide that I should be in charge. My voice is close enough to the voice of the people of Israel, isn't it? Hearing no dissent, Judah took control.

What happened next shouldn't be a big surprise to you. Judah ordered the people of Israel to go and kill a bunch of other people, called Canaanites, in a bunch of other cities. It was the command of God, Judah said.

Judah assembled a big rally, the biggest rally of all time, totally unprecedented. "These Canaanites," Judah said, "they must think we are the dumbest and the weakest and the stupidest people on Earth. On Earth!"

"You know, I read a story. It's a terrible story, but I'll tell it to you. Should I tell you, or should I not?"

# THE TRUMP BIBLE

"Okay, I'll tell you. Early in this century, last century, General Pershing, did you ever hear of him? He was a rough guy. Rough guy. They had a Canaanite problem, and there's a while thing with swine and animals and pigs, and you know the story. They don't like them, and they were having a tremendous problem with Canaanites, and by the way, this is something you can read in the history books, not a lot of history books, because they don't like teaching this, and General Pershing was a rough guy, and he sits on his horse, straight like a ram-rod, and it was early in this century, and this was a terrible problem."

"They were having Canaanite problems, just like we do, and he caught 50 Canaanites who did tremendous damage and killed many people, and he took the 50 Canaanites, and he took 50 men, and he dipped 50 bullets in pig's blood. You heard that, right? He took 50 bullets, and he dipped them in pig's blood, and he had his men load his rifles and he lined up the 50 people, and they shot 49 of those people, and to the 50$^{th}$ person, he said, 'You go back to your people and you tell them what happened.'"

"So, we better start getting tough, and we better start getting vigilant, and we better start using our heads, or we're not going to have a country, folks! We're not going to have a country."

But then, having given his orders, Judah went to his home at Dead-Sea-a-Lago and played some golf.

With Judah gone, some of the people of Israel decided that they had had enough of killing entire cities of people. They didn't want to skewer children with their swords any longer, so they settled in next to the people of Canaan, trying to be neighborly.

Then an angel of God came down, and spoke to the people, saying, "Have you all forgotten your Judeo-Christian values? I thought Judah, I mean God, made it very clear that you were supposed to kill all these Canaanites and smash all their temples, not be nice with them. So, why aren't you spreading havoc and bloodshed, as you have been ordered to do?"

The people of Israel looked at each other, and then back at the angel, and said, "Forget you. We're just trying to get along in peace here for a change. Buzz off."

God was provoked to anger, and started arranging to have the people of Israel killed and sold into slavery for failing to obey his orders to commit more genocide.

God anointed people he called "judges" to go around killing other Israelites, stabbing each other in the stomach, smashing each other's heads with hammers, and hacked each other apart with swords.

Judah kept on playing golf.

This guy Gideon came around, and dominated everyone by waving around his sword, but said to them, "Honest, it is not I who is ruling over you. It's God. Yeah, that's it. It's God."

Then, Gideon's followers gave him all the gold earrings of the people they had killed. Gideon had many wives, and concubines too. "Grab them by the pussy," Gideon proclaimed.

So, the children of Israel saw the great Judeo-Christian morals of Gideon, and decided to place holy books in all the inns in the land in his honor.

Judah was still playing golf.

So, the men of Israel went to Jabesh-gilead and seized 400 young virgin girls, and dragged them to their camp at Shiloah, and forced them to become their wives, according to their Judeo-Christian values.

# 8 TRUMP LAMENTATIONS

Oh my God, how the Tower sits alone. It was once full of people. People came, and ate steaks in the restaurant, and drank the wine, but now, nobody much comes anymore.

That Tower, she's like a widow, or more like an ex-wife. She was a princess once, a trophy wife, but now she weeps sorely in the night, and her tears run down her cheeks, and her mascara is running, and among all her lovers she has no one to comfort her. All her friends have betrayed her, and become her enemies.

But hey, what are you gonna do? I'm not the best husband. Never pretended I was.

Ivana went into an affliction, and no she dwells among the heathen, and she finds no rest. She mourns, because she doesn't come to my feasts any longer.

The doors of the Tower are desolate. The priests sigh about what goes on here, and the virgins are afflicted. Outside, Ivana is in bitterness. The Lord Trump has afflicted her for the multitude of her transgressions. Their children have gone into captivity in the tower, afflicted with the Stockholm Syndrome.

Marla has grievously sinned, therefore she is removed.

All that honored her despise her, because they have seen her nakedness: Yea, she sighs, and turns backward and moves with Tiffany to the West Coast. Her filthiness is in her skirts, and she came down with no comforter.

The adversary has spread out his hand upon all her pleasant things, for she has seen that heathen entered into her sanctuary, the guard who you commanded not to enter. All her people sigh, for the have given their pleasant things for meat.

Does this mean nothing to you? The Lord Trump has afflicted his aides with his fierce anger, making them desolate, fainting throughout the day.

Trump binds the yoke of our transgressions by his hand, to come around our necks, making our strength to fall until we are not able to rise up. It is said that he has trodden under foot all the mighty men in our midst, and has crushed the virgins as if they were grapes in a winepress, but we deny these accusations.

Trump called for his lovers, but they deceived him, despite their non-disclosure agreements and substantial payments from his lawyers. Behold, Trump is in distress, and his bowels are troubled, for everyone has gloriously rebelled against him, and are idiots who don't understand how to do anything.

Let all their wickedness come before the Lord, and unto them, who have done to Trump all their transgressions, for his sighs are many, and his heart is faint, will be delivered the word that they are fired.

I am the man who has seen affliction by the media of the swamp, in its wrath leading me into darkness, and not into light.

Surely against me Bannon has turned, and Sessions has turned his hand against me all the day. My flesh and skin have been made old by Rosenstein, and Comey has broken my bones. Mueller has set me in dark places, as they that be dead of old.

The Washington Post has hedged me about, so that I

cannot escape, and has made my chain heavy. The New York Times has enclosed my ways with hewn stone, and has made my paths crooked. CNN was unto me as a bear lying in wait, and as a lion in secret places.

I was a derision to all my people, and they made songs about me all the day, until Saturday Night live filled me with bitterness, broke my teeth with gravel stones, and covered me with ashes, until I forgot I was a billionaire, and the most successful businessman that the world has ever known, but my money I recall to my mind, and therefore I have hope.

# 9 TRUMP PROVERBS

Actually, throughout my life, my two greatest assets have been mental stability and being, like, really smart. Crooked Hillary Clinton also played these cards very hard and, as everyone knows, went down in flames. I went from VERY successful businessman, to top T.V. Star to President of the United States (on my first try). I think that would qualify as not smart, but genius.... and a very stable genius at that!

Sorry losers and haters, but my IQ is one of the highest – and you all know it! Please don't feel so stupid or insecure. It's not your fault.

A woman I don't know and, to the best of my knowledge, never met, is on the FRONT PAGE of the Fake News Washington Post saying I kissed her (for two minutes yet) in the lobby of Trump Tower 12 years ago. Never happened! Who would do this in a public space with live security?

Lightweight Senator Kirsten Gillibrand, a total flunky for Chuck Schumer and someone who would come to my office "begging" for campaign contributions not so long ago (and would do anything for them), is now in the ring fighting against Trump. Very disloyal to Bill & Crooked-

USED!

A lot of bad things happened on the other side, not on this side, but the other side. And somebody should look into it because what they did was really fraudulent.

CHAIN MIGRATION must end now! Some people come in, and they bring their whole family with them, who can be truly evil. NOT ACCEPTABLE!

This whole Witch Hunt is an illegal disgrace... and Obama did nothing about Russia!

The U.S. cannot allow EBOLA infected people back. People that go to far away places to help out are great – but must suffer the consequences!

I want to thank Steve Bannon for his service to the campaign. He came to the campaign during my run against Crooked Hillary Clinton – it was great!

Michael Wolff is a total loser who made up stories in order to sell this really boring and untruthful book. He used Sloppy Steve Bannon, who cried when he got fired and begged for his job. Now Sloppy Steve has been dumped like a dog by almost everyone. Too bad!

I would like to extend my best wishes to all, even the haters and the losers, on this special date, September 11.

Finally, Liddle' Adam Schiff, the leakin' monster of no control, is now blaming the Obama Administration for Russian meddling in the 2016 Election. He is finally right about something. Obama was President, knew of the threat, and did nothing. Thank you Adam!

Sad to see the history and culture of our great country being ripped apart with the removal of beautiful statues and monuments. You can't change history, but you can learn from it – Robert E. Lee, Stonewall Jackson...

Another false story, this time in the Failing @nytimes, that I watch 4-8 hours of television a day - Wrong! Also, I seldom, if ever, watch CNN or MSNBC, both of which I consider Fake News. I never watch Don Lemon, who I once called the "dumbest man on television!" Bad Reporting.

An 'extremely credible source' has called my office and told me that @BarackObama's birth certificate is a fraud.

Immediately fire back if a savage sicko came to a school with bad intentions. A "gun free" school is a magnet for bad people. If a potential "sicko shooter" knows that a school has a large number of very weapons talented teachers (and others) who will be instantly shooting, the sicko will NEVER attack that school. Cowards won't go there...problem solved. Must be offensive, defense alone won't work! Armed Educators (and trusted people who work within a school) love our students and will protect them. Very smart people. Must be firearms adept & have annual training. Should get yearly bonus. Shootings will not happen again - a big & very inexpensive deterrent.

Reason I canceled my trip to London is that I am not a big fan of the Obama Administration having sold perhaps the best located and finest embassy in London for "peanuts," only to build a new one in an off location for 1.2 billion dollars. Bad deal. Wanted me to cut ribbon-NO!

I will be announcing THE MOST DISHONEST & CORRUPT MEDIA AWARDS OF THE YEAR on Monday at 5:00 o'clock. Subjects will cover Dishonesty & Bad Reporting in various categories from the Fake News Media. Stay tuned! So much Fake News is being reported. They don't even try to get it right, or correct it when they are wrong. They promote the Fake Book of a mentally deranged author, who knowingly writes false information. The Mainstream Media is crazed that WE won the election!

I had to fire General Flynn because he lied to the Vice President and the FBI. He has pled guilty to those lies. It is a shame because his actions during the transition were lawful. There was nothing to hide!

Most politicians would have gone to a meeting like the one Don Jr attended in order to get info on an opponent. That's politics! My son Donald did a good job last night.

He was open, transparent, and innocent. This is the greatest Witch Hunt in political history. Sad!

The Wall is the Wall, it has never changed or evolved from the first day I conceived of it. Parts will be, of necessity, see through and it was never intended to be built in areas where there is natural protection such as mountains, wastelands or tough rivers or water. The Wall will be paid for, directly or indirectly, or through longer term reimbursement, by Mexico, which has a ridiculous $71 billion dollar trade surplus with the U.S. The $20 billion dollar Wall is "peanuts" compared to what Mexico makes from the U.S. NAFTA is a bad joke!

As a very active President with lots of things happening, it is not possible for my surrogates to stand at podium with perfect accuracy! Maybe the best thing to do would be to cancel all future "press briefings".

Rasmussen just announced that my approval rating jumped to 49%, a far better number than I had in winning the Election, and higher than certain "sacred cows." Other Trump polls are way up also. So why does the media refuse to write this? Oh well, someday!

Our country needs a good "shutdown" in September to fix mess!

I heard low ratings @Morning_Joe speaks badly of me (don't watch any more). Then how come low I.Q. Crazy Mika, along with Psycho Joe, came to Mar-a-Lago three nights in a row around New Year's Eve, and insisted in joining me. She was bleeding badly from a face-lift. I said no!

James Comey better hope that there are no "tapes" of our conversations before he starts leaking to the press!

So many positive things going on for the U.S.A. and the Fake News Media just doesn't want to go there. Same negative stories over and over again! No wonder the People no longer trust the media, whose approval ratings are correctly at their lowest levels in history!   #MAGA

My Twitter account was taken down for 11 minutes by

a rogue employee. I guess the word must finally be getting out-and having an impact.

Despite the negative press covfefe.

# 10 TRUMP OBADIAH

Trump is a man of vision, but we have heard a rumor. Someone sent an ambassador to do some negotiating with a foreign country. There is no use in talking to them. We will settle this out our way, sooner or later, so let us rise up against her in battle!

Behold, America is despised and small among the nations. It's embarrassing. We never win any more.

The pride of my heart deceives me, but who will bring me down to the ground?

How are the things of Velnitskaya searched out? How are the secret things of Sergei Millian sought up?

All the men of the deep state conspiracy brought you to the border, but I'm going to build a wall there, and it's going to be so high, you've never seen anything so huge, and Mexico is going to pay for it.

Besides, everybody knows that it was the Democrats who were colluding with Russia, to help get the dirt on Crooked Hillary out. You know it just makes sense! I am accomplishing a lot in Washington and have never had so much fun doing something. They laugh at what our leaders have been. No more!

It reminds me of Alex Baldwin, whose mediocre career

was saved when he began his terrible impersonation me of. IF YOU DON'T HAVE STEEL, YOU DON'T HAVE A COUNTRY!

You should not have entered the gates of our Homeland in our day of calamity, neither should you have looked upon our affliction, nor laid your hand our our substance. I don't care if you were just a baby at the time, nay, not even if you were a toddler, or five years old.

It's time for you to be held responsible for your choices! You should not have spoken so proudly when Obama offered you DACA, though, as John Kelly pointed out, if you didn't do anything then, you were either afraid to come out of the shadows, or just plain lazy. Lazy, yeah.

And they of the south shall remain in Cuidad Juarez, or in Chihuahua, yea, or be deported to Honduras.

And the captivity of this host of children shall be over like a bad dream, because I will give them a path to citizenship, or wait, no I won't, which is to say, yes, of course I will, so long as I get funding for the wall, from Mexico, or from Congress, or of course from Mexico, which is what I have been saying all along.

And saviours shall come upon the Rio Grande from countries like Norway, from whence the right kind of people emigrate, if you know what I mean.

# 11 TRUMPZEKIEL

Now it came to pass in the 15th year, in the seventh month, on the 16th day, the heavens were opened, and I saw visions of God.

And I looked, and behold, an escalator descended from the second floor, a great escalator, a stair enfolding itself, and a brightness was all around it, from the flashing of bulbs, and out of the midst thereof as the color of a ripe citrus fruit, out of the midst of a lobby of marble, there came the likeness of a living creature.

This was its appearance, that it had a likeness of a man, but it had two faces, and held aloft a flabby appendage, flapping with the likeness of a wing, with a tiny hand at its end, and the handrail of the escalator shone with the likeness of burnished brass.

As this creature descended the stair enfolding itself, it turned not, but continued waving its little-handed wing, and I beheld that in great circles surrounding its eyes, the skin was much paler than the color of a ripe citrus fruit, almost in the likeness of a man.

This reminded me that, the other night, I had a dream in which I was driving a car successfully all the way back to my childhood home, until I pulled into the driveway, when for a split second I stopped looking where I was going, and I hit the rear of my mother's car, which was already parked in the driveway, but near the end of it, where I wasn't expecting it to be. Then, in the dream, I was meeting with a therapist who asked me about the dream. I told him that, if he really wanted me to spell it out for him, I would. It was all about my father, who died without passing on even enough money for more than a couple payments on a car. I was engaging in a dream interpretation within the dream I was interpreting. Heavy.

And as it went toward the stage, I heard a sound as of a crowd of sock puppets, paid to applaud the strange creature's descent.

And lo, the spectacle was beheld by all nations, as if all channels felt compelled to witness its drama, though others akin to this creature had received from less time upon the air, and all who beheld the sight, their spirit was inclined to go, and yet they could not look away from the vision, nay, not even to go to the refrigerator.

I fell upon my face, and heard the voice of the one that spake, and the voice said unto me, "Wow. Whoah. That is some group of people. Thousands. So very nice. Thank you very much. That's really nice. Thank you. There's never been a crowd like this."

Then, the voice told me, "Woe to women who sew pillows to armholes! Behold, I am against your pillows!" And I shook my head, and lo, I was in bed, and it was six o'clock in the morning, nearly time to wake up. And I turned to my wife to say, "You would not believe the dream I just had," but observed that her pillow was sewn to the armhole of her pajamas, wherefore I tiptoed out of the bedroom, drove to work early, and have not returned any of her texts today.

# 12 TRUMP NAHUM

I am jealous, and I revenge myself. I revenge myself! I am furious, and will take vengeance on my adversaries, and reserve wrath for my enemies.

Don't blame me. I'm slow to anger. I am great in power. You should see my power. It's tremendous. I am not going to forgive the wicked, because they are very, very bad. I have my way, no matter what the weather is like outside.

I will stand outside and shout at the ocean if I feel like it, until it dries up. If the people don't like me any more, they can languish. Languish!

Who can stand before my indignation? Who can abide in the fierceness of my anger? My fury is like fire – fire and fury. I'll throw rocks at the windows of the White House until they're all broken.

It isn't fair! I'm the President of the United States, and I am still not getting things my way! Nobody told me it would be like this.

I'm a good person, and I know who I can trust, but if people aren't careful, I will unleash a catastrophe, a great big flood of my anger, and even in the darkness my enemies won't be able to hide from me.

What did you think you were doing? You thought you could defy Donald Trump? I will make an utter end of you.

A person who can break everything into little itty bitty pieces is now in your face. Yeah. I'm talking about me. So, watch yourself.

I'm having a parade. A great big military parade, with lots of flags and tanks and big guns and jet airplanes and my soldiers all marching in front of me at my command. My troops will rage down Pennsylvania Avenue, and I shall recount my worthies.

Woe to the bloody city of Washington DC. It is all full of lies and robbery. It's a swamp! I'm going to drain it, and put in my own alligators and swamp reeds, the way I want it.

Because of the multitude of the whoredoms of the wellfavoured harlot, Melania can stay up in Trump Tower in Manhattan for a while, at least until Barron is out of school. I have nondisclosure agreements for everybody if someone wants to cause trouble, and it's my lawyer who will pay for it all. No, I know nothing about it. It's all him.

I have multiplied the merchants above the stars of heaven, and lowered their taxes.

All that hear the bruit of me will clap their hands over their faces and whimper, for upon who has my wickedness not passed continually? Yeah, that's right. Deal with it.

# 13 TRUMP ZACHARIA

Be not as your fathers, whom have cried to me, saying, turn now from your evil ways, and stop tweeting. I did not hear, or hearken unto them, I said.

Issue a press release, they say. Submit it through the office of the press secretary, they say. Blah, blah, blah. You can't say this! You can't do that! Who are these people? Who do they think they are? Do they think that they're going to live forever? I don't think so.

Have I not passed the biggest number of laws by any President ever? Do I not have the biggest approval rating of anyone since Andrew Jackson? Beat that.

Then came the word of the prophet of Fox News saying, I saw by night, a man riding a red horse, and I went up to him, and I said, hey, what's going on? And the prophet of Fox News said he would show me what was going on.

Have you not heard that Barack Obama was not born in Hawaii, as it was said, but in Kenya? No kidding, I said. No way.

Way, said the prophet of Fox News.

And my son, whose name is Junior, talked to an angel, who appearing from the heavens in amongst the myrtle trees, promised to arrange some special help, saying, did you know that I've got some dirt on Hillary Clinton that can help you beat her in the election? Would you like to see it? How about we hold a meeting and we can talk about it, and maybe we can come to an arrangement.

And Junior, in an email that is now held by Robert Mueller, said sure, that sounds great.

And behold, they did meet in Trump Tower, while I was there even just a few floors up, but I never knew about the meeting, and certainly did not go downstairs to talk to the angel with the dirt on Hillary Clinton, for I would never certainly never get involved in anything like that.

And Junior talked to me later, and explained that the whole meeting was really just about helping Russian orphans find nice American homes to live in, and not, as the emails suggest, about trading stolen material for political favors with the Russian government, even though the angel did go back to Moscow and submit a report to Vladimir Putin.

Oh no, I said, how could you think such a thing? Although, now that you mention it, I was jealous of Crooked Hillary with great fury.

I sat in a corner of the Oval Office and mumbled, as Bob Corker announced that he would not seek re-election, for sure this time. And I said, As I thought to punish you, provoked to wrath, and I repented not, so again have I thought in these days. And I threw the remote control at the TV set, and the buttons as they struck the cabinet changed the channel to MSNBC, and now the controls are broken, and I can neither change the channel nor turn off the TV.

And I saw that the idols have spoken vanity, and the diviners have seen a lie, and have told false dreams, for they claim that I did not win the popular vote, and deny that there were millions of illegal votes. They comfort in vain.

# 14 TRUMP MALACHI

There were a whole bunch of other books, too, but reading is hard. It makes us tired, and leads us to want to play more golf. So, yadda yadda yadda…

…lots of smiting…

…and then there was Malachi, who was trying to talk to God, but God kept on rattling on, and what a weariness is it! "Cursed be the deceiver, which has in his flock a male, and voweth, blah, blah blah."

Look, the point is that I am a great leader. I have the greatest record of any leader so far, in all of history, and my name is dreadful among the heathen, okay?

Then, God threatened to spread shit on people's faces. I am not kidding. That's what he said: "I will corrupt your seed, and spread dung upon your faces, even the dung of your solemn feasts."

So what? The liberals, they're going to try to tell you that we can't talk like this. "Oh no, you can't say that!" Says who? I could walk into the middle of Jerusalem and stab everyone I came across, and still, the children of Israel would support me. The pollsters tell me so.

But they tell me, "Judah has dealt treacherously, and an abomination is committed in Israel, for Judah has married the daughter of a strange god." It's fake news, folks. They've stolen the election from me. It's a setup. The Deep State is all stacked against me, and lo, there is a pizza parlor in Washington D.C. that has a secret sex ring operated by Hillary Clinton in its basements, and InfoWars shall return, and discern between the righteous and the wicked, between him that serves me and him that serves me not. Oops, I meant to say him that serves God. God. Yeah, that's what it's all about. God.

I'm with the evangelicals, now, for behold, the day comes that shall burn as hot as an oven, and that's proof enough for me that there have always been fluctuations of temperature up and down. They had hot days in ancient Jerusalem, see, but now they come and tell you that burning coal has made global warming. It's plenty cold here today, you know? I think we could use some of that global warming.

We are going to cut down my opponents like stalks of wheat in the field, and leave behind their remains only, like they're stubble in a field that's been harvested. That's right, fire and fury, because my enemies will be ashes under the soles of my feet on the great and dreadful day when I get the Deep State out of my way and fire Robert Mueller, or, what I meant to say is, when it's the day of the Lord our God! God, yeah. That's what I meant to say.

We're totally going to smite you with a curse, God and I, because it's about love and peace and compassion, and smiting people until they're like stubble and ashes.

Don't say I didn't warn you. Now excuse me. I'm late for my tee time.

# 15 THE GOSPEL OF TRUMP

In the beginning was Fox and Friends, and Fox and Friends was with Trump, and Fox and Friends was Trump. Or maybe Sean Hannity. Joe Scarborough once too, but we'll get to him.

The same was in the beginning with God. Same difference! God, Trump, potato, potahto.

All things were made by Trump and nothing was made without him. Casinos, universities, steaks, reality TV shows, racially-segregated apartment buildings, you name it.

Trump turned around the entire economy, single-handed, in just six months, not that the media would report on it. Fake news! The failing New York Times, on the brink of bankruptcy, won't report on it.

There was a man sent from God, whose name was Donald. He was both the witness of the light, and the light, the true light which lights every man that comes into the world, but which gives some men $200 million dollars of inheritance to bootstrap their way on up, and others something less.

Women? I did try and fuck them. They were married. In fact, I took them out furniture shopping.

Trump was in the world, and the world was made by him and the world knew him not, until he started appearing on television.

He came into his own in Queens, but they received him not in Manhattan, at least not for a few years. He was in the world, and the world was made by him, and knew him by the name that he plastered on everything he came into contact with: Trump!

As many as received Donald Trump, to them he gave power to become his employees, or his contractors, unless he didn't like the quality of their work, in which case, they didn't deserve to be paid. The sons of Trump, however, believe in his name, and are employed as the father by the father, at least when they aren't on safari in Africa shooting large game animals.

For his enterprises were born, not of blood, or of the will of the flesh, nor of the will of man, nor particularly his intellect, but of the name Trump itself, which stands for the ability of a man born to incredible wealth to expand him wealth somewhat, though none may see his tax returns.

And the Trump brand name was made flesh, and then more flesh, and dwelt not among us, for who could behold the glory of his gold-encrusted penthouse apartment, as the only surviving begotten of his father, full of himself in truth.

Trump bared the orange flesh of him, and cried, saying, "I must say that I want to thank a lot of the news organizations here today because they looked at that nonsense that was released by maybe the intelligence agencies, who knows, but maybe the intelligence agencies which would be a tremendous blot on their record if they in fact did that, a tremendous blot, because a think like that should never have been written, it should never have been had, and it should certainly never have been released, and I will say, if the election didn't turn out the way it turned out, they would not be here. They would not be in my office. They would not be in anybody else's office. They'd be building and doing things in other countries, so there's a great spirit going on right now, a spirit that many people have told me they've never seen before, ever."

And of his fullness we have all received.

And they asked him, "What, then?"

And he said, "I think we're going to do a real job, and I'm very proud of what we've done, and we haven't even gotten there yet."

And they asked, "Who are you? What say you of yourself?

He said, "It's all fake news. It's phony stuff. It didn't happen, and it was gotten by opponents of ours, as you know, because you reported it and so did many of the other people. It was a group of opponents that got together, sick people, and they put that crap together. It should never have been, number one, shouldn't have even entered paper, but I think it should have never have been released, but I read what I released and I think it's a disgrace. I think it's an absolute disgrace."

The next day, Mike Pence saw Trump coming and said, "Behold the Lamb of God, which takes away the sin of the world." And Pence said, "I saw the Spirit descending from heaven like a dove, and it abode upon him."

Against the next day after Pence stood with two of Trump's aides, and looking upon Trump as he walked, he said, "Behold the Lamb of God," and the two aides heard him speak, and they followed Trump.

Then Trump turned, and saw them following, and said to them, "What do you think you're looking at?"

They said to him, "Sir, where are you going?" and he said to them, come and see. They came and saw where he was watching InfoWars while eating McDonald's, for it was about the tenth hour of watching.

The third day, the Ivanka of Trump was there, and Trump was called, along with his aides, to Ivanka, and when they wanted wine, Ivanka said to them, "I don't have any wine."

Then Trump said to Ivanka, "What does that have to do with me? It's not time for me to go to bed yet!"

Ivanka said to the White House staff, "Look, whatever he tells you to do, just do it, okay?"

Then, there was set before Trump and his aides six extra large colas, after the manner of refreshment during halftime of the Superbowl, and a tray containing two or three cheeseburgers apiece.

After a while, Trump said to them, give me some more soda to drink, and his aides filled the cups back up to the brim.

After this he went down to Mar-A-Lago, he and Ivanka, and Melania, and his aides, and they continued there many days, for the sabbath of tee time was at hand, and Trump went up to the 9$^{th}$ hole before getting tired, and found on the green some diplomats from foreign countries, selling contracts with Trump businesses, and he drove them all back to the clubhouse, and poured out the changers' money, and turned the tables, and performed the art of the deal, and said to them, "Take these things hence to the Trump International hotel in Washington, D.C, where my father's house has some expensive conference rooms for rent."

Trump's aides remembered that it was written, "The zeal of your house has eaten me up", and they asked him, "What's going on, sir, that you are sending people with government meetings with you to rent rooms in businesses with which you promised to cease involvement?"

He said to them, "I am the greatest President ever to sit in the Oval Office, and verily, I say unto you, hereafter you will see heaven open, and the angels of God ascending and descending upon me," and he spoke of the temple of his body, and his aides believed the talking points, though Trump had deviated from them.

Trump did not commit himself to them, however, because he didn't particularly care about any one else, and but expected that they should testify on his behalf, asking each, "Are you on my team?"

There was a man of the FBI, named Robert Mueller, a Republican administrator with extensive prosecutorial experience, and he came to Trump by memo, and said to him, "I would like to interview you under oath."

Trump answered and said unto him, "Verily, I say unto you, except a man be loyal to me, he cannot see me in private."

Mueller said to him, "How can you refuse to speak to a legally-established investigation?"

Trump answered, "Except a man be elected President of the United States, he cannot claim executive privilege. That which is of the President is above the law, and can pardon himself. Marvel not that I said unto you that I would not speak with you, for sure, I will talk to you under oath, with the approval of my lawyers, of course."

And lo, the wind blows where it will, and Trump's lawyers heard the sound of his statement, and could not tell where he was coming from, or where his mind was going, as is of everyone who is born into a multimillion dollar fortune.

Wherefore, his lawyers answered, and said unto Mueller, "How can these things be? Surely Trump will not speak to you, under oath or in any other form."

And Trump said, "If I have told you earthly things, and you don't believe me, how will you believe me when I tell you about my alternative facts? For I so love Vladimir Putin that he gave his only hacked information, that whosoever should receive that information should not vote for Hillary Clinton, but have everlasting trust in the Republican Party, for everyone that tells fake news hates the truth, and never is interviewed on Fox News, lest his deeds should be reproved, but my deeds may be made manifest, that I am the only one who can Make America Great Again."

When therefore Trump heard how the Pharisees had

said that Hillary Clinton had baptized more disciples than he, though Trump himself saw unprecedented millions out on the National Mall, a crowd for his inauguration larger than any had ever seen before, he turned off the television set, and yelled at Sean Spicer, and shouted unto him, "I have more burgers to eat than you yet know of! Don't say to me that there are yet four years, and then comes our victory! I won! I'm the President, and you're not!"

And everyone in the room believed because of his own fear for being yelled at next.

When Trump was come out of his tantrum, there was a certain corporate CEO whose business was ailing at the Pentagon. When he heard that Trump was holding a business roundtable, he went unto him, and besought him that he would restore special funding for the canceled weapons project, and heal his business, for it was at the point of death.

Then Trump said to him, "Except if you see me restore funding to your weapons program, though it be wasteful to the point of extravagance, you will not believe that America is Made Great Again, and have my back. Go away, your weapons program lives."

This was not the first business miracle that Trump performed, when he was come out of his tantrum, yea, not even less than a hundred, for there were a great multitude of corporate CEOs willing to make a deal in return for their silence.

After this there as a man who did not carry his bed with him, but did carry the Confederate flag with him to Charlottesville, Virginia, and verily, a second flag with a swastika, too, and therefore did the Jews persecute him, because he had waved these flags in procession with others carrying torches and shouting, "White pride!"

With him marched a great multitude, seeking the more to kill the Jews, and the African-Americans, and the Hispanics, and the Muslims, and the Liberals, running them down with their cars, for attempting to make themselves equal with their white Christian masters. They were a burning and a shining light through the streets of Charlottesville, and the ghosts of the Confederacy were willing for a season to rejoice in this light.

Then Trump was asked by the Pharisees, "What shall we do?" And he said, "I can of mine own self do nothing, as I hear, because there is fault on both sides. It's all fake news! If you believe not my words, how will any believe your writings! Look in Fox News. Look on Breitbart, for they testify of me! I have come in my father's name. He provides me with business contacts, and free education, and lo, though he sends me off to a military boarding school, yet he gives me a two hundred million dollar inheritance."

After these things, Trump went to his country club at Bedminster, and there he sat with his aides, and had a very nice meal, but when it was time for desert, the steward came and said, "I'm sorry, sir, but we're all out of crème brule."

Therefore, Trump called the manager, and he said unto his aides, "Let's order some delivery."

And the manager entered into a helicopter that flew to Manhattan, and landing on Trump Tower, was stocked with twelve baskets of crème brule.

And Trump took the crème brule, and sent some over to the executive table, where his friend the Governor was sitting, and when the Governor's wife had seen the miracle that Trump did, said, "This is of a truth that should come into the world," and cracked the crust with her spoon to get to the soft custard.

The next day, Trump was out on the 5$^{th}$ hole, and did bank a shot to the left, so that his ball could not be seen on the green, nor anywhere in the rough, or even in the sand banks. Yet, when Trump came to stand next to the flag, to consider his options, his ball appeared just two feet from the hole, though none had seen it there just a second before.

Trump looked to his aides, and said unto them, "Murmur not among yourselves. You all saw me make this great shot, didn't you?"

And all among them agreed that they had, and this they called the miracle of the 5th hole.

On the way to the next hole, Trump and his aides came upon a Democrat, who asked of them, "Can I not speak to you of health care? For my constituents have great need of medical attention, and yet you seek to destroy their access."

And Trump pointed down to some flowers growing along the path, and said, "Consider the lilies of the field. They have no health care plan, but look! They're getting along fine. In the same way, you shouldn't worry about having health care, because God will take care of everything if you just believe hard enough. So, if you think about it, the fact that you're sick kind of implies that you're an unholy slacker. I mean, lilies aren't exactly the highest achievers. They could have been something, if maybe they got off their asses and worked for it a little bit. Just saying."

Upon returning to the clubhouse, a gathering of Pharisees was waiting for him, and among their number, a man whose limbs were possessed by demons, and Trump reproached the man, imitating the strange movements of his arms, and the other Pharisees began to murmur, saying, "This is a hard thing for you to do. Who can watch this?"

When Trump knew in himself that the Pharisees murmured at him, he said unto them, "What? Do I offend you? Do you have a problem with that?"

"I am the most intelligent man ever to hold this office, but there are some of you that believe it not." For Trump knew from the beginning who they were who should betray him.

And he said, "There is no one else who can fix things. I alone can do it."

From that time on, John Kelly held his face in in his

hands, and many in the crowd walked no more with him.

Then said Trump to his aides cowering in his shadow, "I made you! Did I not choose Little Reince? I have chosen you all, and yet one of you is a devil!"

He spoke of Steve Bannon, for he it was that should betray him.

And Donald Jr. said unto Congress, "There are some of you here who believe not. For my father knew from the beginning those among you who would not believe, and who should betray him. Therefore, I say to you, there are none who can come to me except through my father."

From that time forward, many in Congress walked back, because they did not understand what the hell Donald Jr. was talking about.

And many among the Republicans in Congress marveled, asking themselves, how can the President know so much, having only attended military academy and business school?

And Trump rebuked them, saying, my doctrine is not mine. It is merely what Fox News has sent me.

And Bannon would not walk in Jewry, because he was sure that the Jews meant to kill him, which was not at all antisemitic of him. Oh, no, not at all.

And Trump said, did not Reagan give you the law, and yet none of you keep the law? Why are you going around trying to stab me in the back and kill me?

And Republicans in Congress thought to themselves that Trump was sounding kind of paranoid, but said nothing out loud, for the sake of party unity.

Then Trump put his finger up in the air, and shaking it back and forth, told them, "Yet a little while I am with you, but soon I shall go back to bed with some ice cream, and thither you cannot come. Then you will look for me, and will not find me."

Many of the Republicans, upon hearing this, said, "This is a true prophet. Yea, for though he may have many flaws, he will lower taxes on corporations and endeavor to abolish ObamaCare, under which we have been gravely afflicted with coverage despite pre-existing conditions.

But others said, "I don't know. Can a true Republican come from New York City? Never a President spake as spake this man."

So there was a division among the Republicans because of him, but they decided to keep quiet about it, and show a united front, because, after all, who would want to see a Democrat in the White House?

Later in the morning, after Donald Trump woke up, watched Fox and Friends, and had some executive time back in bed, he came to the Oval Office with a bowl of olives, and all the aides he had left came to see him, and he sat down.

And the aides brought unto Trump a woman taken in adultery by him, and when they had set her in the midst, they said until him, "Master, this woman was taken in adultery by you, in the very act, and your lawyers paid her $130,000 to remain silent. Now, the Christian family values you told Republican voters that you believe in dictate that you should not have sex with anyone but your wife, especially when your wife, your third wife, had just given birth to your youngest son. But what say you?"

This they said, tempting him, that they might have to accuse him. But Trump leaned forward in his high-backed leather office chair, and colored in between the lines of the drawings in the book of pictures that had been placed upon his desk, as though he heard them not.

So when they continued asking him, he lifted himself up and said unto them, "Do you remember Lyin' Ted Cruz? Well, when he used a picture of Melania from a G.Q. shoot in his ad. I told him, 'Be careful, Lyin' Ted, or I will spill the beans on your wife.' Well, I didn't spill the beans on Lyin' Ted's wife, but my political adviser Roger Stone sure did, and on Lyin' Ted, too. Five mistresses at once! I love that story. Best issue of the National Enquirer ever!"

And again, Trump sat down at his desk and concentrated on coloring between the lines.

And when they heard what Trump had said, they were convicted by their own conscience, ad went out one by one, until even to the last, Trump was left alone, except for the woman standing in the middle of the Oval Office, staring at him.

"What?" Trump bellowed. "I deny it. It never happened. Now get out of here, and sin no more!"

When the woman had left, his advisors came back into the Oval Office, and Trump said unto them, "I am the most successful businessman in American history. He who follows me will be totally set, so successful! But watch out! If you double cross me, you're out!"

Then Trump turned to the least among them, and asked, "Hey you, what's your name? Never mind. You're fired!"

Then the aides around him were all astonishment at the wonder of the power of Trump, and asked, "Who the hell do you think you are?"

And Trump said to them, "I told you who I am. Listen next time, and don't bring any more whores in here, unless, you know what I mean. Hey, it's only because I tell you the truth that you don't believe me."

As he spake these words, many who did not understand what he was talking about decided to believe him nonetheless.

As Trump was watching television with his aides the next Monday morning, they saw a story about a man who had been disabled from cerebral palsy from birth, and could not afford health insurance to pay for his medical care.

And his aides asked him, saying, Master, whose fault is this, that he should be sick and yet unable to receive necessary therapy to ease his suffering?

Trump answered by bringing his arm up suddenly to his chest in imitation of the man's tremors, saying, "Doh!

Doh! I don't know anything! I can't get medical care! Doh!"

When he had spoken, his advisors looked nervously amongst themselves for a moment, and then they laughed.

I told you before – he that comes into the United States not by the special perks available to rich foreign businessmen willing to make special "investments", but crosses the border some other way, the same is a thief and a robber.

But she who is an eastern European fashion model shall receive an Einstein grant for her special abilities, which she shall give to the nation by walking around looking fabulous.

And when she obtains special legal permanent resident status for her parents, as she goes before them, and they follow her, knowing her voice, that shall not count as chain migration, because, you know, she's my wife.

This parable spake Trump unto his followers, but they understood not what things they were which he spake unto them.

Then Trump spoke unto them again, and said, "No really. Everyone who came before me is just a thief, a criminal, but the voters didn't care. They voted me in with the largest popular victory in American history!"

The Democrats are running away. They're giving up, because they're scared of me and sore losers, and all they have to say is "Russia!"

There was a division among the Republicans who heard him, and many of them said, "Trump is insane! Why are we listening to him!"

Others said, no, these aren't crazy words. He knows exactly what he's doing. He won the election, didn't he?

One of his interns, a campaign donor's son, "Why are not these moneys cut from the National Endowments for the Arts and Humanities, and from the EPA, and NOAA, and the national parks, and transportation, and Housing and Urban Development, and many other agencies, given to the poor?"

Then said Trump, "Leave that money alone, for against the day of my re-election it has been re-allocated to my corporate allies, for the poor you always have with you, but me you will not have always."

And Trump went all across the United States, preaching in stadium, regarding all manner of sickness and disease among the reporters writing about his speeches, and calling upon them to be jeered.

And seeing the multitudes in one section of the stadium, while ignoring the empty seats in the rest, he said, "Look at this crowd! There has never been a crowd this size, but don't expect the media to report on it!"

And he opened his mouth, and taught them, saying,

Shitholes are the poor, for they are low energy.

Shitholes are they who mourn, for I don't think their sons were really heroes, and besides that, I think they're Muslims.

Shitholes are the meek, for they will not inherit the earth. I already own it. That's mine!

Shitholes are those who hunger after what's right, for there is a lot blame on both sides, believe me.

Shitholes are the merciful, for they are rewarding failure.

Shitholes are the pure in heart, because they lack the courage to grab some pussy.

Shitholes are the peacemakers, for they don't win anything anymore.

Rejoice and be glad, because your reward is in heaven. Rewards for trust fund kids and big corporations will be served here on earth, in Line 1. Be sure to bring your Trump loyalty rewards card.

You are the coal of the earth, but if that coal has lost its market value, where will you find jobs! Apparently, coal is good for nothing after all, but to be cast out, and trodden under the feet of men leaving Appalachia. Sorry, but hey, at least the War On Coal is over, right?

Your are the light of the world, carrying tiki torches through the streets of Charlottesville, North Carolina.

Think not that I have come to drain the swamp. I have come not to destroy, but to inhabit.

You have heard it said by the Establishment, thou shall not kill, but I say unto you that whosoever was protesting during a rally when I was kid, they would have been brought out on a stretcher. I tell you what: Go ahead and throw stones. I'll pay the legal fees.

And whosoever is angry with his brother, and whosoever says, you fool, well, remember that the other side has plenty of problems too.

Therefore go to DonaldTrump.com and leave there thy gift, and go thy way. Verily I say unto you, you shall by no means come out thence, till thou hast paid the uttermost.

You have heard that it was said by the Establishment, thou shall not commit adultery, but I say unto you, do you have proof that I committed adultery? It's my word against hers, and hers, and hers, and hers.

Hey, consider this: Whoever looks on a woman to lust after her has already committed adultery with her already in his heart, so why not go all the way?

If your right eye offends me, pluck it out and cast it away from you, but I just went to the eye doctor, and he said that I have the healthiest eyes he's ever looked at. Really. I have a signed document that says so. I'll keep my eyes, I think.

It has been said that it is profitable that one of your members should perish, and not that your whole body should be cast into Hell, but my member is working just fine. Believe me.

Again, you have heard it said by the Establishment that you should not forswear yourself, but screw that. Like Sarah Sanders pointed out, I have already won in arbitration against Stormy Daniels. I swear it's true – and she has sworn an oath not to contradict me.

## THE TRUMP BIBLE

You have heard it said, an eye for an eye and a tooth for a tooth, but that's no way to run a business. I drive a hard bargain: You have to pay two eyes for an eye, and two teeth for a tooth. That's the art of the deal.

Besides, I say to you, whoever slaps you on the cheek, take him to court and sue him until he pays! And if any man sues you at the law to take away your coat, just refuse to pay him, and then settle it out of court with plausible deniability.

You have heard that it's been said that you should love your neighbor and hate your enemy, but I say unto you, watch your back and hate your neighbor too. Bless them who bless you, and curse those who curse you. Am I right?

If you love them who love you, well, what do you get out of that? Don't they love you already? So, move on! Next!

Take heed that you don't do alms where other people can see it. Just say that you're going to make a big donation. Everybody loves that. They eat it up. Then, they'll go on and pay attention to the next big thing, and you don't actually have to make a donation. You've already gotten all the good PR you need! Do not even the Republicans do the same?

With the measure that you mete out punishment, so you will be measured by. People are watching, so bomb the shit out of them!

And if you're looking in someone else's eye, and you notice that they've got a little speck in there, don't let them hog all the attention. So what, they've got a speck. Big deal! The beam in my eye is the biggest of anyone around, the biggest beam of all time! You have never seen a beam like the one I've got in my eye. That's because while other people are busy running around plucking out their eyes, so afraid to cause offense, I keep both of mine. That's the only way to get a really big beam like mine. Huge!

When you pray, don't be like the hypocrites who pray in secret, for they love to go into little private places and pray behind closed doors, where they can't get any publicity for praying. What are they trying to hide, do you think?

When you pray, be like me, and pray standing out on the corners of the streets, or in the big stadiums where you hold rallies and have people waiting at tables to take financial donations. Otherwise, why do it. Verily, I say unto you, I shall have my reward.

When you pray, if you can at all manage it, pray on television at the National Prayer Breakfast, which, it is true, is not really a national event, but just happens in one place, and is actually put together by a shadowy right wing religious order that calls itself The Family, which does not at all sound like a cult, no, no, no. But get up at the podium, and give a loud speech about how much you love praying, and make sure that your best side is facing the camera as you do so, because if you have no reward of your Father which is in heaven, you have to get what you can right now, right? Well, we will see.

And when you pray, don't forget to ask for this: Forgive us our debts, as we take others to court to gain the best advantage over our debtors, because, if you're not taking full advantage, you might as well not be in business.

And remember, if you forgive men their trespasses, then nobody will remember what's wrong with them. You have to repeat your message if you want people to get it. Repetition is everything. Repetition is everything!

Now, the heavens send rain on both the just and the unjust. Unfair! So, what are we going to do about it? The death penalty for drug dealers is a discussion we have to start thinking about. I don't think we should play games.

Yes, it's true that I eliminated funding for the White House office designated to deal with the opioid crisis, but I never did polling on that. I don't know if it's that popular or unpopular. But, these people are killing our kids, and they're killing our families, and we can't just keep setting up blue-ribbon committees with your wife and your wife and your husband, and they meet and they have a meal, and they talk, talk, talk, talk, talk, and two hours later, then they write a report.

Who ever read a report? Not me!

Lay not up for yourselves treasures in heaven, because nobody accepts mana from heaven when the bill comes. For where your treasure is, there will your heart be also. I love treasure!

No man can serve two masters. So, choose the winner! Serve Trump! You cannot serve Trump and mammon, and look, nobody even understands what mammon is, so why would you serve that?

Therefore I say to you, take no thought for what you shall eat or what you shall drink, or what clothes you shall put on. When you're a celebrity, people give you freebies all the time. Is not life more than food and clothes, anyway? Yes, it certainly is. Focus on real estate!

Which of you by just thinking about it can add one cubit to his stature? You can't! But me, I've got the biggest hands. Just look at them. Believe me, I don't have a problem in that department.

I say to you that even Solomon in all his glory was not arrayed like me. Did Solomon have any golf courses? I don't think so.

Seek first to put your name all over your properties, so that everyone knows who owns them, and then all these other things shall be added unto you. Then, tomorrow will take thought for all the other things on its own. No worries. Hakuna Matata!

With what judgment shall you judge, and with what measure shall you mete? Choose carefully, because when you bring the hammer down, people need to know about it.

Don't throw that which is worthy to the dogs, and don't cast your pearls to the pigs, either. Keep the riff raff out by charging a high membership fee. Then, just knock, and the door will open for you. The world will be your oyster!

And hey, if a man asks for a fish, what man would give him a serpent? To tell the truth, I have no idea. We'll see. We'll see. Just keeping you on your toes. Trick question. Serpents and fish, geez. You should have seen the look on your face when I asked you that one.

So, I'm not perfect. Never pretended to be, though I am ranked by all objective historians as being the greatest president ever to sit in the Oval Office.

But, let's say I'm no good. Let's say I'm evil. Hey, I know how to give good gifts to my children, right? Nobody can argue against that.

Hey, but seriously, when all those Mexican rapists and M-13 gang members walk up to the border, they ought to have the common decency to enter the USA through the straight gate where Homeland Security is waiting for them, because narrow is the way that leads to the good life, and few there are who find it.

Now, do men gather grapes of thorns, or figs of thistles? No. Real men hire somebody to do that for them. They're job creators.

Some people complain that I'm not doing right by the environment. They say that I'm letting industries come in to wreck the national forest. But, I say, if it's a national forest, who am I to tell anyone in the nation that they can't have a piece of it? Every tree that doesn't bring forth good fruit should be cut down and cast into the fire. I didn't make that up. It's the holy word. Swear to God. Look it up, and think about it – what kind of sickos don't want to cut down trees that don't bear good fruit, right? By their fruits you shall know them.

Many in the Republican National Committee will say to me, Mr. Trump, Mr. Trump, have we not come to your rallies and endorsed you, and clapped at your speeches? In your name, have we not cast out the dreamers? In your name, haven't we passed legislation to let Wall Street investment firms cook up whatever schemes they want without any regulations to limit their greed.

And then I will profess unto them, I never knew you. Depart from me. Losers!

And it came to pass, when Trump had finally stopped talking, the people were astonished at his doctrine, for he taught them as one having authority, and not as one who has wasted his time studying things and reading a lot of books, or national security briefings.

When Trump was come back into the Mar-A-Lago clubhouse from the golf course, great multitudes followed him.

And behold, there came a sick man worshipping him, saying, Mr. Trump, if you will, can you finally pass some legislation establishing good health care coverage? When you were campaigning, you promised that when you became President, you would create the best health care system in the whole world, and everybody would have great coverage. So, how about it?

And Trump said to him, are you kidding me? Go your way, and take a shower. Don't you know I'm a germophobe? Gross.

And Trump slathered a thick layer of hand sanitizer over each of his large and masculine fingers, only rubbing it off with a hot moist towel brought by his wait staff, rolled, not folded.

And Trump said to nobody in particular, this man is not worthy to come under my roof, for I am a man with authority, with soldiers under me, and I say to them go, and he goes, and to another come, and he comes, and to them all, do this, and they do it.

So, why shouldn't I have a parade? They do it in North Korea and China! They do it in Russia! I want a parade. A big one, with tanks and airplanes, and all our nuclear missiles, and big guns that go bang, bang, bang! Where is my parade?

So that which was spoken by Esaias the prophet was fulfilled, and Trump took our infirmities and bare out sicknesses. Never before were so many sicknesses laid bare. Bare sicknesses aren't pretty either, let me tell you.

And behold, at one of his rallies, Trump's aides brought him before a journalist sick of the palsy, and Trump said, "Oh, the poor guy, you've got to see this guy! He's going like, uhhh, I don't know what I said. Uhhh, I don't remember!"

And Trump reminded them, nobody adds an new piece of cloth onto an old piece of clothing, except for hoboes. I dressed up as a hobo for Halloween once. Also, no one should put new wine into old bottles. That's why I'm against recycling.

While he said these things, behold, there came a certain man, and begged Trump, please, come and lay your hand upon my daughter. So, look, Trump didn't know she was underage. Nothing wrong about that, is there? But Trump straightly charged his aides, saying, see that no one knows anything about this, and compelled them to sign non-disclosure agreements, and there was nothing at all suspicious about that.

And when he had called unto him his Cabinet, he gave them power against unclean spirits, to cast them out, such as those named Priebus, or Scaramucci, or Omarosa.

Do not scrimp on your journey, he told his followers, nor travel in economy class, for the workman is worthy of his meat. Therefore, fly you in first class, lest the hoi polloi ask you uncomfortable questions or in other ways challenge your authority. And in whatsoever city or town you shall enter, inquire which hotels in it are worthy of five star ratings, and there abide until to go thence.

Behold, I send you forth as sheep in the midst of wolves: Be ye therefore wise as serpents, and harmless as doves, and like a spoon made for mixing metaphors.

Now, beware, because you shall be brought before governors and special counsels for my sake, for a testimony against me, but when they issue you a subpoena, take now thought how or what you shall speak, for it shall be given you in that same hour by text message what you shall speak, for it is not that you speak, but that the executive privilege prevents you.

And you shall be hated of all men for my name's sake, but he who endures to the end shall be saved. Here's my plan: When they come to serve you a subpoena in one city, just flee to another, and leave a message with your receptionist saying that you're out on the road, and your phone has run out of juice.

Remember, the disciple is not above his master, so shut up and do what I tell you. Don't worry about it, therefore, for it's like Hope Hicks says: There is nothing covered that shall be revealed, and nothing hidden that shall be known.

But, whosoever denies my role in this whole Russia hoax thing before Robert Mueller, him I will also deny when I am called in to testify.

Now, when Paul Manafort heard in the prison the works of Trump, he sent for two of his lawyers, and said unto them, "Do you have my back, or do I have to flip for a plea deal?"

Trump answered and said unto him, "He who has ears to hear, let him hear, but I can always pardon you if things get hard and you have not lamented."

At that time, Trump woke up early, at 11:00 AM, and made some deals with foreign businessmen and governments to have them stay at his hotels. But when the muckrakers saw it, they said to him, "Behold, your business is involving you in emoluments, and that is not lawful."

But Trump said to them, "Have you not heard what Crooked Hillary did, when she set up a private email server? Why aren't you writing about that?"

And when he was departed thence, he went into the Oval Office and gave Russians classified information that revealed the identities of secret intelligence sources, and subsequently, some of them were killed with poisons linked to the Kremlin.

And Trump said to them, "Big whoop. Who is there among you who, when you have Russian diplomats come to your offices, don't give them a classified secret or two? So, it is lawful for me to do it, too."

Then, Trump withdrew himself into his bedroom, and put his head under the covers, and charged that his whereabouts should not be made known. And alone in the darkness, Trump muttered, "He who is not with me is against me, and whosoever speaks a word against me, it shall not be forgiven him, neither in this world, nor in the world to come."

While Trump yet talked to himself, behold, his daughter and his son-in-law stood outside the bedroom door, desiring to speak with him. Then his Chief of Staff knocked on the door, saying, "Ivanka and Jared would like to speak with you."

Then Trump shouted through the door, and said, "Who is my daughter, and who is my son-in-law?"

But he answered before John Kelly could say anything, and pointed at the television, saying, "The people at Fox News are my family, for whosoever shall do my will, they are like my daughter or my son-in-law."

Later that day, Trump flew out to a golf course, and sat on a bench by the 13$^{th}$ hole, and he said many things, including a story about General Pershing, who was a rough guy.

And he said, "People think we are the dumbest and the weakest and the stupidest people on Earth. On Earth! You know, I read a story. It's a terrible story, but I'll tell you. Should I tell you, or should I not?"

And the crowd roared with hunger for the terrible story, so Trump said, "Okay, whoever has ears to hear, let him hear. They had a terrorism problem, and there's a whole thing with swine and animals and pigs, and you know the story. They don't like them, and they were having a tremendous problem with terrorism, and by the way, this is something you can read in the history books, not a lot of history books, because they don't like teaching this, and General Pershing was a rough guy, and he sits on his horse, straight like a ramrod, and it was early 1900s, and this was a terrible problem. They were having terrorism problems, just like we do, and he caught 50 terrorists who did tremendous damage, and he took the 50 terrorists, and he took 50 men and dipped 50 bullets in pig's blood. You heard about that? He took 50 bullets and dipped them in pig's blood, and he has his men load up their rifles and he lined up the 50 people and they shot 49 of those people, and the 50th person, he said, you go back to your people and you tell them what happened, and for 25 years there wasn't a problem. We've got to start getting tough and we've got to start being vigilant and we've got to start using our heads or we're not gonna have a country, folks! We're not gonna have a country."

But a man named Jason D. Schwartzman stood up and pointed out that the story of General Pershing putting bullets in pig's blood is nothing by a myth. It never happened.

And Trump said, "Not true. Not true. Totally false. Fake news, Little Jason! Let me tell you what's going to happen. I'm going to send forth my people across America, and they will gather everything that offends me, and cast them into a furnace of fire, and there will be wailing and gnashing of teeth, and then the good people of America will shine forth!"

And there were those in the crowd who looked uncomfortable, and seeing this, Trump called out, "What? You have a problem with that? I say let them burn! Those of who have ears to hear, let them hear!"

And some in the crowd were astonished, and muttered to themselves, "Wherefore is this man saying these nasty things?" But the better part of the crowd roared with approval, and so the rally went on as planned.

And when Trump's advisors were gathered at the end of the rally, they were hungry. So Trump ordered ten Big

Macs with large fries, to be delivered to the Oval Office, and they did all eat, and were filled, but felt a little bit queasy afterwards.

But the Surgeon General arrived, and asked, why are you giving such unhealthy food to your staff? They won't be able to work long on a bad diet like this.

And Trump answered, saying, "Hear me and understand. It isn't what goes into your mouth that's unhealthy, but that which comes out of your mouth. So, stop saying these ugly things to me. Come on and have some fries. Hope Hicks doesn't want hers."

And when his staff had licked their fingers clean of special sauce and salt, Scott Pruitt stood up and told them, "Do you know that the environmentalists were offended when I told them this? Well, it's the truth, anyway. Our heavenly Father commands that every plant which He has not planted shall be pulled up. We have a lot of pulling to do before the Earth is holy and bare again."

And the environmentalists also with the scientists came, and desired that Trump would show to them how their measurements of climate change were wrong.

And Pruitt stood up again and said unto them, "When it is evening, and the sky is red, then you know the weather will be nice, but in the morning, it will be foul weather because the sky is red. Hypocrites, you can look in the sky and see the signs of weather to come, but can you discern the signs of the times? A wicked generation seeks signs of the weather, and there shall be no signs given to them, except by the sign of the prophet Jonas!"

And the scientists and environmentalists were not sure what point Pruitt was trying to make, and so, without saying anything, they departed. And Pruitt declared that he had won the climate change debate.

When Trump came to his pollsters, he asked them, "Who do people say that I, the greatest President of all time, am?"

And they said, "Well, some say that you are a great

disruptor, and others, that you are a populist, or just another one of the billionaires who was born rich and has never had anybody with enough courage ever to contradict your to your face."

And Trump said unto them, "Yeah, yeah, but who do you say that I am?"

And the senior pollster said, "Uh, you are the greatest President of all time, sir."

And Trump said to him, "You are really skilled at your work, you know that? For though your numbers may not have revealed these results to you, you have been able to sort them out with sophisticated interpretation. I tell you what. I'm giving you a new nickname. We're going to call you The Rock from now on. Keep up the good work, and I'll give you the keys to the kingdom."

From that time forth began Trump to show his advisors that he must go to Jerusalem and move the U.S. embassy there, because it was part of the ancient prophecy with the red heifer, and they understood not, but Mike Pence told them to watch Kirk Cameron's version of Left Behind, and then they would understand.

Then a few days later, the pollster now known as The Rock took Trump aside, and began to rebuke him, saying that the poll numbers showed that Trump was not the greatest President of all time after all, and that, in fact, he had the lowest approval ratings of any President in American history since the time when opinion polls began.

But Trump turned and said unto The Rock, "Get behind me, Satan! You are an offense to me, for you only measure the opinions of little men!"

Then said Trump to his advisors, "Whoever of you who loses his life for my sake shall find it!"

And the advisors of Trump shifted uncomfortably in their chairs and sought to change the subject of conversation.

And after six days, Trump traveled to California to look at the samples of the border wall that had been created to block off the United States from Mexico, and while yet he looked, behold, a bright cloud overshadowed him, and behold a voice out of the cloud said, "This is my pick for the design of the border wall, with which I am well pleased!"

And when the advisors saw that Trump had merely cupped his hand over his mouth in such a way as to cast his voice using a hidden walkie talkie, they covered their faces and were sore afraid.

And Trump came and touched them, and said, "Arise, and be not afraid." And when they had lifted up their their eyes, they saw no walkie talkie, but Trump only.

And as they came down to the parking lot to get back into the presidential limousine, the advisors asked, "Didn't you say that before the wall could be built, that Mexico must first pay for it?"

And Trump answered and said unto them, "Truly, Mexico will first pay for the wall, but I say unto you, Mexico has already paid for the wall, but it was in secret, and has done whatever I asked, because I am that good at making deals."

And when they had returned to the White House, and the multitude of reporters in the press room, a certain journalist said, "You promised you were going to fix health care, and everyone was going to have the best health care coverage ever, but I brought this question to your advisors, and they could not tell me of anything you have done to actually put this health care plan in place."

Then Trump answered and said, "Oh you faithless and perverse generation, how long shall I be with you? How long shall I suffer you?"

And Trump summoned his advisors to him, and they asked, "Why can we not fix health care? You told us we had the power to do so."

And Trump said unto them, "It is because of your unbelief, for I say to you that if you have trust in me even the size of a grain of mustard seed, you could move mountains, and nothing would be impossible for you. So, what's wrong with you? Go remove yourself to the White House lawn and sit there on the grass until I call you back inside!"

And when the advisors were allowed back inside, Trump told them, "If your right eye offends me, pluck it out and cast it away from you, but I just went to the eye doctor, and he said that I have the healthiest eyes he's ever looked at. Really. I have a signed document that says so. I'll keep my eyes, I think."

And Trump's advisors looked nervously at each other until one of them asked, "Sir, I think you told us that story already, a few times."

And Trump said that no, he had not.

And Trump's advisors let the matter drop, because they knew that he was merely repeating himself, and the only way to get him to stop was to allow the story to go all the way to the end.

And two hours later, Trump ended his story by saying, "I tell you, wherever two or three of you are gathered in my name, there I am in the midst of them, unless you are meeting with Natalia Veselnitskaya, or with Sergey Kislyak, or with a Russian oligarch. Then, I am not there. You never saw me, or told me about the meeting, right?"

Then came Sarah Huckabee Sanders to him, and said, "Sir, how many times shall you give me false information to the press corps, and I shall defend it as if it is the truth? Till seven times?"

Trump said unto her, "I tell you what. Not seven times. Until seventy times. Today. Seventy times today, and the same for tomorrow. And the day after that."

And Trump departed from thence, and came nigh unto the Trump Tower in Manhattan, and sat down there.

And great multitudes of channels came unto him through the television set, and yet there was nothing on.

Everywhere but Fox News, the journalists and other liberals came, and tempting desired him that he would show them a plan to fulfil all his promises. So Trump turned off the TV, and called for his aides, saying unto them, "Go down to McDonald's, and straightaway you shall find a deal for Shamrock Shakes, for it is nigh unto March. Bring two of them unto me.

And if any man says anything about you ordering two Shamrock Shakes for me, you shall say, my boss has need of them, but one is for his son Barron. All this was done, that it might be fulfilled which was spoken by the prophet, saying, thy satisfaction comes unto you, sweet, but also kind of minty.

And the aides went and did as Trump commanded them.

Then went the lawyers for Robert Mueller, and took counsel how they might entangle Trump in his talk, and they sent out to him a message, saying, Mr. President, we know you are true, so we would like to interview you under oath about your activities with the Russian government of Vladimir Putin during the attacks of 2016. Tell us, therefore what you think.

But Trump perceived their wickedness, and said yes, I will be happy to talk to Robert Mueller, and I'll do it under oath, too. Of course, I have to talk with my lawyers first.

When they had heard these words, they marveled, and left him, and went their way.

And then Trump's lawyers sent out a message saying that he would only talk if it was guaranteed that he would only be asked questions in response to which he could not possibly lie, so that he should avoid perjuring himself.

And when Mueller's lawyers had heard that Trump had put put them to silence, they were gathered together. Then one of them said to Trump, what is the highest law of the land?

Trump said unto him, Make America Great Again. This is the highest law of the land, and the second is very similar to it: Pay as little tax as you can, because anyone who knows what they're doing in business understands that.

Then Trump asked them, if Ivanka is my daughter, how come I look young enough to date her? Sit at my right hand, until I make you my footstool!

And no one was able to answer this with even a word, and for the rest of the week, no one dared to try to ask Trump any more questions.

Then Trump fell into a strange mood, and began to tell odd stories about servants getting drunk and hitting each other, and about ten virgins carrying lamps to go and meet some guy they married, the same guy, but getting lost in the dark, and about people arguing about money and goats.

His smartphone was kept in its secret place that day, though verily his advisors told him it was lost, though Trump told them that if they didn't find it for him right away, through would go away into everlasting punishment.

And it came to pass that day that Robert Mueller's lawyers returned, asking again to speak to Trump, who locked his doors, and finding his smartphone hidden in amongst a pile of boring daily security briefings, tweeted in anger, asking: Are you come out as against a thief with swords and sticks to take me?

And Mueller sought witnesses against him, and many testified, saying that Trump had told them about getting help from the Russians, but they were all false witnesses. All of them were lying, and their evidence was fake. Only what Trump had to say was true. There was no collusion!

And Trump would not leave his bedroom for three days, locking the door shut and remaining silent as if his room were a sepulcher, not even to receive a plate of fresh, warm chocolate chip cookies and milk. So his advisors set a watch outside his door.

But behold, at the end of the third day, Melania came to try the door, and heard a great sound from within the chamber, as if from an earthquake, and the Secret Service, opening the door, declared that Trump was not to be found at all within, and a single window was open, its curtains blowing in the breeze.

And Franklin Graham, upon hearing this news, spread news of the miracle, declaring that Trump had risen, ascending to the heavens to be with the angels. But Robert Mueller gave large money unto the Secret Service, saying, tell everyone that his advisors came and stole Trump away while they slept, lifting him out of the window and flying him away to his golf course in Scotland.

And this fake news is still commonly reported until this day.

# 16 TRUMP ROMANS

Vain in their imaginations, Democrats won't stop complaining. Professing themselves to be wise, they became fools, and can only now place blame in others. Being filled with all unrighteousness, fornication, wickedness, covetousness, maliciousness, full of envy, murder, debate, deceit, malignity, whisperers, backbiters, haters of God, despiteful, proud, boasters, inventors of evil things, disobedient to parents, without understanding, covenant breakers, without natural affection, implacable, unmerciful liberals can only talk about the negative.

Sad!

You're inexcusable, all you people who judge me. Whatever you judge bounces off of me and sticks on you. Like glue!

To them who are contentious, and do not obey the truth, with indignation and wrath, tribulation and anguish, remember goes the victory. I'm President, and you're not!

You know what else? Men and women have turned the natural use of women into that which is against nature. Men with men are working that which is unseemly. Why not do what's natural, and just grab them by the pussy? That's why I will allow no transgender people in the military.

You know what's inexcusable? Judging people. I hate people who judge people. You know what else is rotten? Lack of forgiveness. I will never be able to get over that.

At this point, I'm supposed to talk about circumcision, but let's be honest, okay? It makes me feel kind of squeamish just thinking about it. It's like I keep telling you. I'm a germaphobe.

While I'm talking about being honest, isn't honesty overrated? I mean, look, talking as man, let every man be a liar, for if the truth has more abounded through my lie unto the glory of God, why yet am I also judged as a sinner? It just doesn't make any sense.

And look, all this talk about me breaking the law, well, we all know that whatever things the law says you have to do, it only says to those things who are under the law, and the President is not under the law, but has executive privilege. So, let every mouth be stopped.

I am justified by faith without the deeds of the law. So, the law is void.

I see another law in my members, warring against the law of my mind, and bringing me into the vaptivity of the law of sin. Who shall deliver me from this nonsense?

Besides that, all the world is guilty before God, so I'm no worse than anyone else.

No one understands. No one.

Everybody has gone off down the wrong path, and all the businesses have become unprofitable, and nobody does any good any more. No, not even one person is doing anything good.

I just killed a man. I put a gun up to his head, pulled the trigger, now he's dead. Mama, life has just begun, but now I've gone and thrown it all away.

Nothing really matters to me.

What? Do you think you're better than me? I don't think so. Let's just stop all this talk about right and wrong, and who colluded with who.

And really, do I boast? No. I am the most humble man you will ever meet.

Now, my children are my heirs, and therefore, joint-heirs to the presidency, and able to pardon themselves, for I reckon that the sufferings of this present time are not worth it all, and what is the point of being President if you can't have a bit of fun, for the whole world groans and works in pain otherwise.

If we hope for things that we don't see, well, we'll see. We'll see what happens.

Hate what's evil. I get that.

Don't be lazy in business. Right.

Those who persecute you, remember, revenge is a dish best served cold.

Mind the high things, and don't condescend to men of low estate. Be conceited in your wisdom.

Recompense evil for evil.

If it's possible to be peaceful, well, okay, but if they who threaten you do it just one more time, then the gloves go off. It's time to get tough. Avenge yourself, and give place to wrath, for it is written, vengeance is mine, and I will repay what you've done to me.

If your enemy hungers, don't feed him. If your enemy thirsts, don't give him anything to drink. Heap coals of fire on his head.

Everybody is subject to the powers that are bigger than they are. So, whoever resists big powers is in rebellion against God, and are damned.

Rulers are only terrible to people who are evil. So, only the evil are afraid of my power. Do what I tell you to do, and you'll have my praise, but beware, for I am the minister of God's wrath, a revenger to execute those who do me wrong.

Let us walk as in the day, in rioting and drunkenness, in chambering and wantonness, in strife and envying. Make provision for the flesh, to fulfil the lusts thereof.

Happy is he that does not condemn himself in that

thing which he allowed himself to do. You know what I'm talking about. I'm talking about that thing. You remember. That thing. Right.

Don't let all my goodness be spoken evil of. It's time to overhaul the libel laws, so that the fake news can be punished, and reporters put in jail for what they have said about me. Lock them up!

Those who believe in me, they can eat whatever they want. The rest of you can only have salad.

# 16 TRUMP TIMOTHY

Memo to John Kelly: Has anyone noticed that there isn't a single guy in my Cabinet named Timothy, Tim, or even Timmy? We could have a Little Timmy. Have Jared and Ivanka look into that for me. I'm sure an opening will come along sooner rather than later.

It has been said that my business deals are illegal, that they are emoluments, whatever that means. The law is not made for a righteous man, though, but for the lawless and disobedient, for the ungodly and for sinners, for unholy and profane, for murderers of fathers and murderers of mothers, for manslayers, for whoremongers, for them that defile themselves with mankind, for menstealers, for liars, for perjured persons, and anything else that contradicts my ideas about how to Make America Great Again. The law is fine if it's used lawfully, but face it: The Democrats use the law illegally, so it doesn't apply. Besides, I can't obstruct justice. I am justice.

Now, on the whole Stormy Daniels thing, and the the Access Hollywood tape, remember what the apostle Paul said? Let the woman learn in silence with all subjection, but I suffer not a woman to teach, nor to usurp authority over the man, but to be in silence. So, let them be silent!

Paul said that men shall be lovers of themselves, covetous, boasters, proud, I thankful, without natural affection, trucebreakers, false accusers, fierce, traitors, heady, highminded, creeping into houses, leading captive silly women laden with sins. Sounds good to me!

It has been said that a woman who lives in pleasure is dead even while she's alive. These younger women, they learn to be idle, wandering around from house to house. They're not only lazy, either. They're tattlers and busybodies. They're talking about things that that they shouldn't be talking about. So, let's refuse to listen to these profane and old wives' fables, all right? Shun these profane and vain babblings!

A bishop must be blameless, the husband of one wife, vigilant, sober, of good behavior, given to hospitality, apt to teach, no striker, not greedy of filthy lucre, but patient, not covetous, one who rules well his own house, not a novice lifted up with pride... but then, I'm not a bishop, am I?

People who rich in this world should not be not highminded. Godliness is content with great gain, and I have had great gain. That's why people say that I am the most godly man you will ever meet. Believe me.

# 18 TRUMP CORINTHIANS

So, there were these two Corinthians. That's the whole ballgame, the whole shebang.

What? What did I say?

Oh, well, second Corinthians! Well, excuse me! I guess that's what they teach you at Liberty University: What matters is that you're trained to say Second Corinthians, instead of two Corinthians. That's what matters, right?

Right. So, when I say I'm going to bomb the shit out of people, grab women by the pussy, that's not really a big deal. No, and all those women who I had to settle out of court with who accused me of rape and sexual assault, if you want to get technical, maybe I had a lapse in judgment there. But hey, actually, the evangelicals didn't push me on that.

I said "two Corinthians". Wow. I am so sorry.

I mean, I came here to you people at Liberty University, founded by Jerry Falwell, who said that HIV was God's judgment against gay people, but who am I to judge, right?

I told you, that as President, I would provide special to Christianity over all other religions. I can say that, I don't have to be politically correct. Right?

I mean, forget about the separation of church and state. Forget the First Amendment. I know what matters. Christians first!

But then, I made a mistake. No, it wasn't when I said that prisoners of wars are losers. You had no problem with that. It wasn't when I spread rumors about Ted Cruz's father assassinating John F. Kennedy. I mean, what's a little false witness between friends? You get that. No harm, no foul.

Did I invite the Russians to commit a crime, hack into American computers, to help me win the election? Sure I did, and you, my audience at Liberty University, you were understanding. You kept your eye on the prize. Big prize. Never seen a bigger one.

I have to say, and I mean this, the people of Liberty University, and evangelicals everywhere, you've been very understanding of me, very Christian, when I tell the people at my rallies to go and beat up protesters. You understand that I say these things out of love and a faithful heart, ok?

You joined me in refusing to judge David Duke, because who are we to judge the Grand Wizard of the Ku Klux Klan? Who among us has not slipped a little bit, and accidentally put a white robe on while walking around at night, carrying a torch, calling for the establishment of a nation for white people? We all have our regrets, don't we?

The evangelicals didn't have a problem with me calling Mexicans a bunch of rapists.

You didn't mind when I went around to my apartment complexes, and set the policy that black people were not allowed to rent from me and my dad. It's an evangelical thing. It's a Southern thing. Some people don't understand. Right?

So, you people at Liberty University have stood by me, through thick and thin. Thank you. Together, we have done some amazing things. We have stopped the War On Christmas dead in its tracks. Two bullets right between its eyes.

Oh, also, we're working together to make sure that nobody, not even that bunch of smarmy kids from Parkland, Florida, are going to take away our guns. From my cold dead hands, right? Right?

We know that if you can't carry around an AR-15 rifle at school, it's not America. That's why Jerry Falwell Jr. has called me "one of the greatest visionaries of our time". He's right. I am. It's true!

I was touched when Mr. Fallwell said, "Mr. Trump lives a life of loving and helping others as Jesus taught in the New Testament." And look, here it is again, in the New Testament all over again.

So, you didn't complain when I cut funding for programs for the poor. The poor are always going to be poor, after all, but the coal industry, well, coal companies need our help, which you understand.

But, you know, I made a mistake. I hurt your feelings.

I said "two Corinthians" instead of "second Corinthians".

I have to tell you, I don't know what was going through my mind.

I could give you an easy excuse. I could tell you that the campaign trail has been exhausting, and I haven't been getting enough sleep. I could tell you that it was just a slip of the tongue.

Giving you an excuse like that, it just isn't enough, is it?

Evangelicals were really mad at me, and I understand. When I said "two Corinthians", it was unforgiveable, wasn't it? It's okay. We can say that. What I did was unforgiveable. The worst of the worst.

What I'm hoping is that you can find it in your hearts to forgive me anyway, and give me a second chance to be the great Christian President you know I can be, chosen by God to lead the world on the path to righteousness...

...except for the shithole countries, right? I mean, there is no hope for them. Why should we care about them?

PEREGRIN WOOD

# 19 TRUMP COLOSSIANS

You know, sometimes you feel alone. You feel alienated. You feel like you've got enemies all around.

You know what? I'm happy to suffer that way. You want to be my enemy? Forget reconciliation. Bring it on.

I have been put in charge. I'm the President, and that doesn't always mean I'm nice. I want you to know, there's going to be a great conflict in store for you.

I'll tell you this, in case someone comes around with enticing words, beguiling you and stuff. You have to know how to make a deal. Not many people do. I do.

People come to you, and they've got these big ideas, and they think that they can lie to you. It's kind of a tradition for them. That's wrong. Very wrong.

Don't let them intimidate you. That's weak. You work on Sundays. You work on weekends. That's how you get things done Don't relent, because your work now is just a shadow of what you're going to achieve.

When I say work, what I mean to say is delegate responsibility. Make sure that the people working for you understand: This is a 24/7 position you're in. The buck stops with you.

People come to me all puffed up. They think they're

going to put one over on me. They don't know who they're going up against. I use all the tools available to me. I've got malice, blasphemy, filthy communication coming out of my mouth, I don't care. Whatever it takes to win.

You want to be merciful, kind, humble, meek? Not in business. You've got to be tough.

Alright. Let me give you an example. I want some stealth F-18s. I want them at a low price. They tell me, Mr. Trump, there's no such thing as a stealth F-18. I say back to them, no, there isn't, and maybe that's the problem! So now, bang! I've got a stealth F-18 program where none existed before. That is how you get things done.

You're not going to get what you want unless you tell people what you want, and you have to tell them. Don't ask. Tell them, and they will obey you.

I tell people, wives should submit to their husbands. That's it. Submit. Just do as you're told. There's nothing more than I love than women, so long as they've got a beautiful piece of ass but they are far worse than men.

Oh, husbands should love their wives when they're around, if you know what I mean, but love isn't sharing. Husbands are in charge. The biggest mistake I made with Ivana was taking her out of the role of wife and allowing her to run one of my casinos in Atlantic City. The problem was, work was all she wanted to talk about. It was just too much. I will never again give a wife responsibility.

Nobody has more respect for women than I do, but if you want to win a woman, you have to move forward, even if you get smacked.

There was this woman Louise. She worked for me back in the 1970s and 1980s. Whenever she got feeling too good about herself, and felt like challenging me, I took out this picture of her, from when she was fat, and showed it to her. Reminded her she's not so perfect after all. You have to treat them like shit.

I have days where, if I come home, and I don't want to sound too much like a chauvinist, but when I come home, and dinner's not ready, I go through the roof."

What you don't want to do is buy your wife any nice jewelry. Why would you want to give her negotiable assets, if things go south? You need to set those limits from the start.

On prenuptial agreements, there are basically three types of women and reactions. One is the good woman who very much loves her future husband, solely for himself, but refuses to sign the agreement on principle. I fully understand this, but the man should take a pass anyway, and find someone else.

Another kind of woman is the calculating woman who refuses to sign the prenuptial agreement because she is expecting to take advantage of the poor, unsuspecting sucker she has in her grasp. Then there's the other kind of woman, who will openly and quickly sign a prenuptial agreement in order to make a quick hit and take the money given to her.

I made a deal with Ivanka. She was 17 and doing great. She made me promise, swear to her that I would never date a girl younger than her. So, as she grows older, the field is getting very limited, but all the woman on The Apprentice flirted with me, consciously or unconsciously. That's to be expected.

Children need to obey their parents in all things, too. This starts with fathers knowing who they are. There are a lot of women out there that demand that the husband act like the wife, and there are husbands who actually listen to that.

If I had a different type of wife, I probably wouldn't have a baby, you know, because that's not my thing. I'm a really great father, but there are certain things you do and certain things you don't. It's just not for me.

Melania takes great care of the child without me having to do very much. Pregnancy is a wonderful thing for the woman, but it's certainly an inconvenience for a business, and whether people want to say that or not, the fact is that it is an inconvenience for a person that is running a business.

I mean, I won't do anything to take care of the children. I'll supply funds, and she'll take care of the kids. It's not like I'm going to be walking the kids down to Central Park. Right, like I'm going to be walking down Fifth Avenue with a baby in a carriage. It just didn't work.

Often, I will tell friends whose wives are constantly nagging them about this or that, they're better off leaving and cutting their losses. I'm not a great believer in always trying to work things out, because it just doesn't happen that way. For a man to be successful, he needs support at home, just like my father had from my mother, not someone who is always griping and bitching.

Workers too, it's their duty to obey everything their bosses to tell them to do, and to be happy doing it. Happiness should be enough, which is why I recommend that restaurants take the tips from wait staff. Workplace safety protections cost too much too. Safety is nice, but you've got to cut costs, right?

Like I've always said, remember my bonds!

## 20 TRUMP TITUS

A leader must be blameless. So, if I'm self-willed, soon to anger, violent, and greedy for lots of money, hey, don't blame me!

I hold fast to what I've taught, and I convince people to go along with what I want quite easily. There are a lot of people though, who can't stop talking. They think they sound so great. They give these unruly lectures that go all over the place. I can't understand a thing they're saying. They're probably all a bunch of liars.

That's why I rebuke people sharply. Otherwise, how are they ever going to get things right?

Here again, I have to talk about the Jews. Don't give heed to Jewish fables. For people like that, nothing is pure. Even their minds are defiled. They profess that they know God, but they're abominable and disobedience and reprobate in everything.

I know it's not popular to say these things, but the Bible says to speak and rebuke people with all authority without anyone despising you.

So, let's talk about what makes sound doctrine. God, this bores me, but here goes.

Let the old men be sober, grave, temperate, faithful,

charitable and patience. I'm not really an old man yet, though, so thankfully, I don't have to worry about it.

Old women, likewise, need to behave themselves, and not accuse men falsely. Women age faster than men do, too, so they need to be extra careful.

Sound speech that cannot be condemned doesn't accomplish much. If you are never ashamed of what you say, and never say anything bad, then you're never going out on a limb, are you?

Keep this in mind: You should make yourself subject to the power of the President. You should obey all his government offices. Show some respect!

Everybody's foolish, disobedient, and seeking out lusts and pleasures some of the time, living in malice and envy, hateful, so on the whole, I think I'm doing about as well as would be expected.

It's like I told you: It's not by works of righteousness that we're going to be saved, so being nice to people isn't really the point.

Avoid striving about the law, for it is unprofitable and vain.

When I shall send Melania down to you, be diligent, and join me at Mar-A-Lago, for I have decided to stay there for the winter.

Toodle-oo!

# 21 TRUMP JUDE

My beloved fans, you have to fight for what the Republican Party once stood for, because there are certain people, and you all know who I'm talking about, who have crept in unawares into the GOP, who were members of the party, but didn't believe. They were just liberals in disguise, Republicans in name only. They turned the party of Ronald Reagan into a weak shadow of its former self, denying the only true cause of the Republican Party. Reince Priebus couldn't do his job.

Then, the RNC, which was not on my side, illegally put out a fundraising notice saying Trump wants you to contribute to the RNC. We know better than to trust the RNC. So cute! They do not treat me well, and then they use my name, without my knowledge, to raise money for themselves.

These filthy dreamers hate America. They just don't like it. They feel like we need to apologize for who we are. It's true! They're ashamed of their own country. Can you believe it? They speak evil of the proud working people who made America Great Again.

It's very sad that Republicans, even some that were carried over the line on my back, do very little to protect their President.

They think you're just a basket of deplorables, just like the Democrats do. They don't know what they're talking about.

They changed the rules. You know why they changed the rules? Because they saw how well I was doing, and they didn't like it. I know the rules very well, but I know it's stacked against me by the establishment.

How is it possible that the people of the great State of Colorado never got to vote in the Republican Primary? Great anger - totally unfair!

Watch out for them, because they have gone the way of Pocahontas, and Crooked Hillary. When you have a rally, like this one here today, so huge, they come in and they put on a red cap with you, raging, foaming, wandering around like lost stars. We're going to name names.

We're going to have an awards show, for the most weak willed politicians, the murmured, complainers, with their mouths speaking great big words, thinking that they have the upper hand against me. I warned you, didn't I, that there would be people who would mock me, and go after what they think is best for themselves? I told you, and look now.

They wrote a letter, saying that the party should cut funding for my campaign. I said then, the Republican National Committee needs to take control of this situation, and quickly. Well, look who's the President now. It's my party now, and maybe not everybody is going to get an invitation.

Na, na na na na na na, na na na na...

## 22 TRUMP REVELATIONS

I've been thinking about some things, lately, and realized that there's a lot people don't know about me. I'm not the guy you see on TV. It's time that I share my story, and one of the things that people don't realize is that I don't like attention. Hate it. I've been trying to stay out of public attention for years.

Another thing: The baseball cap. Top designers brought me purple hats, sun hats with floppy brims. I told them, no way. We need red, I say, because people are seeing blood.

There is chaos in the streets. This is bad, folks. Everyone is wailing. But that's in the streets. Up above the streets, everything is fine. Peaceful. You could hear a pin drop.

It's like I told Tony Schwartz: Take what you see, and write it in a book. Write the things which you have seen, and the things which are, and the things which shall be hereafter. Did I tell you, that book was nominated for a Nobel Prize for business? Yeah. It's true. I had to tell the Nobel committee that I didn't want to be considered. They were disappointed.

Hey, look, I turned around and saw seven golden

candlesticks. I thought, gold. Okay. I could put that on a lot of things. I called my designer. I said, bedazzle the whole penthouse with gold. The whole thing. Luxury!

There was someone standing in the middle of the candlesticks, and was distracting from my view as I tried to take a picture of it with my smartphone. I had my assistants take him outside.

I know your work. I know how you can't bear all these evil people. There are all these people who say that they're your friends, but they're not. They're all just a bunch of liars.

Are you sorry yet? I want you to beg for forgiveness. If you do, I have some work for you, because you know what you and I share? We hate the same people. That's right. Our hate brings us together. I can say these things, but nobody else wants to.

To anyone who wants to hear, tell them that anybody who comes to my meeting, they can have some really nice steak. From the best cows. Forget Angus. This stuff is really tender. You won't believe it.

Okay, this is going to be hard for you to hear, but I've got some stuff to say about Jews. They're not going to support me because I don't want their money.

What? Don't get angry at me. Sure, I kept a copy of Hitler's Mein Kampf on my bedside table, but it was my friend Marty Davis from Paramount who gave me a copy of Mein Kampf, and he's a Jew. What? He's not a Jew? Don't bother me with details. Who's a Jew, who's not a Jew? You think you get to decide these things?

I tell you, I've got black accountants at Trump Castle and at Trump Plaza. Black guys counting my money! I hate it. The only kind of people I want counting my money are short guys that wear yarmulkes every day.

The point is, I promise you that I'm much smarter than Jonathan Leibowitz - I mean Jon Stewart, who, by the way, is totally overrated. The point is, there are these Jews who say they're Jews, but they're not, and they are from the synagogue of Satan. I'm going to make them come and worship at my feet. There. I said it. What?

I know what you've done, and I know where you live. Don't forget that, because I have a few things against you. Among them is that you have made a safe place for some of those people I hate.

Also, you have been repeating what those women say against me, to teach and seduce my servants. As if! Just take a look at them. They're so ugly, do you think I would ever touch them?

But look, let's talk about adultery. I'm a great businessman, but I haven't always been the best husband. I admit that. My attitude, though, is that people who commit adultery have to go into great tribulation, except if they say they repent. Then, it's okay. Just say you're sorry afterwards. That's the important thing.

On this pro-life thing. I was reading where Jesus himself once said, "I will kill her children with death." This was about women who were fooling around on their husbands and got pregnant. No kidding. Look it up.

If you stick with me, and you're loyal, I'm going to give you a lot of power, okay, and you can rule with a rod of iron. You know what you can do with that rod of iron? You can smash a lot of pots until they're just these little splintery bits. I used to do that with my father's favorite pots when he was out of town, but he never traced it back to me. Don't tell.

I'm going to come onto you like a thief. A thief, I said, but I don't know when exactly. Still, watch out.

There's an open door of opportunity before you, but you have little strength. You're weak. You have low energy. It's like you're lukewarm. You aren't hot. You aren't cold. Pick a temperature!

So, I say, I am rich, and increased with goods, and have need of nothing. So, I give people advice. First, bring me some of your gold. See, you have to invest in yourself. Enroll in Trump University, and I'll teach you myself all of my secrets of success. Okay, well, there are some things, a lot of things only available at the higher levels of enrollment. Sure, it's not actually a university per se, but you get the picture. Look, if you don't want to be successful, that's fine. Don't enroll. See if I care.

So, I had this weird dream last night. There was this door up in the sky, and there was this thing talking to me, but it was a trumpet. The trumpet said, come here, Donald, and I'll show you some things from the future!

I thought, okay, the future. That's good. So, the trumpet took me to this place where there was a big throne up in the sky, and there was a rainbow in back of it, and some emeralds in it. It kind of reminded me of the throne I have back at home, if you know what I mean.

So, there was also a lot of thunder and lightning, which was not very comforting, and seven lamps burning, and a bunch of really nice crystal. High class. Very sturm und drang.

I looked around, and there were these animals. One was a lion. Another was a baby cow. What do you call them? A calf, right. And the third had a face like a man, so then I wondered, well, if it has a face like a man, isn't it a man, but it wasn't. I don't know how I knew that, but I did. It was a dream. The fourth was an eagle. Okay, except, and this is the strange part, they each had six wings and had a lot of eyes on them. Right. That's how I knew that guy wasn't really a man.

You ever had a dream like that?

Let's talk about reading. Really, there are these snobs at the New York Times, and they preach at you about it. Oh, I'm so literary, they say in a loud voice? Who is worthy to read my book? Nobody, I tell you, no matter where the are, can open those books. Nobody can. You know why? They're boring.

The crown is given to conquer. It's not there so you can have blue ribbon commissions, where people sit and talk and talk and do nothing. Power is given to people, and it's not there so you can just sit around in peace. No. The point is, you kill one another, those who stand against you. Right? I didn't make the rules. I just follow them.

Okay, but here's the thing. You have to know the price of your commodities. How much wheat can you get for a penny? How much barley? How much oil? Commodities trading is the key to success.

I'm sorry. Where was I? I got distracted for a bit there. Right. Kill one another, because there are a lot of people saying, and they're powerful people, when are we going to get to judge and avenge our blood? How long are we going to have to wait? People say wait, rest, but no. We've been waiting too long.

When things get bad, it's going to be the kings of the earth, the great men and the rich men, the chief captains of industry, mighty men, who have a safe haven. You have to be prepared, that's all.

So, there have been some bad wildfires in California. It's not climate change, I can tell you. That's a hoax made up in China. Things burn. What are you going to do.

They say that the drinking water in Flint isn't any good. A third part of the rivers are dirty, and people are dying because of bad drinking water. Okay. I get it. People are upset. You want to know what the real problem is, though? Excessive regulation. If you want to set up a business, you have to go through all this paperwork. Clean water this! Clean water that! That's what makes me sick.

So, I'm not the biggest reader. You know that. Give me an executive summary, I say. So, this guy I met once, he's a genius. He said, you don't have to read to learn. Just consume the knowledge. Literally. No, listen, it's true! He came to me with this little open book, and he told me to eat it, I did, and I'm telling you, I never ate something so delicious. A bit of heartburn afterwards, sure, but it tasted great. Try it some time.

The nations are angry. They're always angry at the United Nations. Talk, talk, talk. They should be judged, or at least have their budget cut.

Have you ever seen one of those science fiction movies where the people who make it have a lot of special effects technology, and they can make anything appear on the screen, but they don't really have a storyline? I saw this movie like that the other day.

These directors put all kinds of things into the movie, like a giant pregnant lady with two wings, running from a giant snake that was spitting water at her, and a dragon, and a creature with ten horns. Why ten horns? Two is enough. They made a big cat monster run around, but with feet like a bear's feet, and I thought, what kind of cat can run around with big fat bear's feet? It doesn't make sense. Where was the story?

Yes, I want a story. Is that too much to ask for? Don't tell me it's all metaphor, or that truth is relative. That doesn't make any sense. It's just multiculturalism.

Sometimes, people talk, and they have a lot to say, but the repeat themselves. This movie was like that. They kept on talking about the mouth of the dragon, and the dark mark, and stuff like that, scene after scene, but it never went anywhere. Boring!

A horse! A horse! My presidential seal commemorative golf course putting green signs for a horse! Oh, look. Here come four.

Our slogan, when we start running in, can you believe it, just two years from now, is going to be Keep America Great – exclamation point!

I mean, look at all we've accomplished! Nobody can argue that this isn't great. The greatest America has ever ever been. So great it hurts.

So, cut to the end. Yes, that's really it. The Trump Bible ends with some talk about weird dreams. Why should it be any other way? I'm tired of writing. Need a nap.

This is the end of the book, and if anyone adds onto this, that's trouble. I'll sue him. Don't say I didn't warn you.

# ABOUT THE AUTHOR

Peregrin Wood was born in a crossfire hurricane, just 15 miles from Grover's Mill, the place where Martians first touched down in their invasion of the Earth back in 1938. True story, though Crooked Hillary doesn't want to talk about it! Sadly, Mr. Wood's birth certificate has never been examined by an independent auditor. Some people are saying that means he can't run for President, and that he was really born in Kenya to a squadron of fundamentalist Islamic Communist terrorists. Is that true? Is it just alternative facts? Well, we are going to have to look into that. We'll see. We'll see.

Made in the USA
Columbia, SC
10 November 2024